Creamy Dip for Fruit

Guests appreciate finding healthful options—like this fresh beauty—on appetizer menus. To make the dip lower in fat, use Neufchâtel cheese in place of cream cheese and opt for low-fat sour cream.

Prep: 15 minutes   **Chill:** 1 hour

- 2 8-oz. pkg. cream cheese, softened
- 2 8-oz. carton sour cream
- ½ cup packed brown sugar
- 2 tsp. vanilla
- 4 to 6 Tbsp. milk
  Assorted dippers (such as cherries, sliced apple, pear, banana, and/or strawberries)

1 In a mixing bowl beat cream cheese with an electric mixer on low speed until smooth. Gradually add sour cream, beating until combined. Add brown sugar and vanilla; beat just until combined. Stir in enough milk to make a dipping consistency. Cover and chill in the refrigerator at least 1 hour before serving.

2 To serve, transfer dip to a serving bowl. Serve with assorted fruits.

Makes 16 servings

Per serving: 189 cal., 16 g total fat (10 g sat. fat), 44 mg chol., 103 mg sodium, 9 g carbo., 0 g fiber, 3 g pro.

Dilled Hummus with Vegetables

Plan on about one cup of fresh vegetables per serving for dipping in this delicious Middle Eastern bean dip.

Prep: 25 minutes   **Chill:** up to 3 days

2 15-oz. cans garbanzo beans (chickpeas), rinsed and drained

½ cup tahini (sesame paste)

⅓ cup lemon juice

2 Tbsp. olive oil or vegetable oil

4 tsp. snipped fresh dill or 1 tsp. dried dill

½ tsp. salt

⅛ tsp. cayenne pepper

4 cloves garlic, minced

Assorted vegetable dippers (such as broccoli florets, carrot sticks, and red sweet pepper strips)

1 In a blender or food processor combine garbanzo beans, tahini, lemon juice, oil, dill, salt, red pepper, and garlic. Cover and blend or process until mixture is smooth, stopping and scraping sides as necessary. Cover and chill for up to 3 days. Stir hummus before serving. Serve with vegetables.

Makes 10 (¼-cup) servings

Per ¼ cup dip with 1 cup vegetables:
209 cal., 10 g total fat (1 g sat. fat), 0 mg chol., 401 mg sodium, 24 g carbo., 7 g fiber, 8 g pro.

To tote: *Transport in an insulated cooler with ice packs. Transport vegetable dippers in an airtight bag or container.*

The Potluck Cookbook

200 RECIPES FOR EVERY GATHERING AND EVERY NIGHT

Meredith® Print Advantage
Des Moines, Iowa

The Potluck Cookbook

Waterbury Publications, Inc.
Des Moines, Iowa

Copyright © 2010 by Meredith Print Advantage
Des Moines, Iowa.
First Edition.
All rights reserved.
Printed in the United States of America.
ISBN: 978-0-696-30070-7

All of us at Meredith Print Advantage are dedicated to providing
you information and ideas to enhance your home. We welcome your
comments and suggestions. Write to us at: Meredith Print Advantage,
1716 Locust St., Des Moines, IA 50309-3023.

Pictured on cover:

Super-Easy Chocolate Bars,
recipe on page 245

Ham Balls in Barbecue Sauce,
recipe on page 152

Italian-Style Spaghetti Squash,
recipe on page 156

Best-Ever Chocolate Cake,
recipe on page 261

Tuna-Noodle Casserole,
recipe on page 179

Crunchy Caramel Apple Cake,
recipe on page 259

Chicken and Orzo Casserole,
recipe on page 66

table of contents

Thai Chicken Wings with Peanut Sauce, page 32

Chapter 1

Boastful Beginnings

Crunchy Cracker Snack Mix

Customize this snack mix by substituting some of your favorite bite-size crackers. Also, if you like another type of nut, substitute it for the mixed nuts.

Prep: 10 minutes   **Bake:** 25 minutes   **Oven:** 300°F

- 4 cups bite-size cheese crackers
- 5 cups snack sticks
- 3 cups pretzel twists
- 2 cups mixed nuts
- ½ cup butter or margarine, melted
- 1 7-oz. envelope cheese-garlic, Parmesan, or Italian dry salad dressing mix

1 Place cheese crackers and snack sticks in a large roasting pan. Bake in a 300°F oven about 5 minutes or until warm. Stir in pretzel twists and nuts. Pour melted butter over all. Sprinkle with salad dressing mix; stir to coat.

2 Bake for 20 minutes more, stirring once. Spread snack mix on foil to cool. Store in an airtight container for up to 1 week.

Makes 13 cups (fifty-two ¼-cup servings)

Per serving: 108 cal., 7 g total fat (2 g sat. fat), 5 mg chol., 217 mg sodium, 10 g carbo., 1 g fiber, 2 g pro.

To tote: *Transport in an airtight container.*

Caramel Snack Mix

This crunchy concoction is perfect for parties, a terrific tailgating tote-along, or kid-pleasing after-school snack. In a small bag tied with a pretty ribbon, it's a welcome hostess gift.

Prep: 15 minutes   **Bake:** 30 minutes   **Cool:** 30 minutes   **Oven:** 300°F

- 1   12-oz. box (12 cups) crispy corn and rice cereal
- 1½   cups mixed nuts, cashews, or almonds
- ½   cup packed brown sugar
- ½   cup light-color corn syrup
- ½   cup butter
- 2   cups chocolate-covered raisins, chocolate-covered peanuts, or semisweet or milk chocolate pieces

1 Preheat oven to 300°F. In a large roasting pan combine cereal and mixed nuts; set aside.

2 In a saucepan combine brown sugar, corn syrup, and butter. Cook and stir over medium heat until butter is melted and mixture is smooth. Pour over cereal mixture; stir gently to coat.

3 Bake, uncovered, for 30 minutes, stirring twice. Remove from oven. Spread mixture on a large piece of buttered foil; cool for 30 minutes. Break into pieces. Stir in chocolate-covered raisins. Store in an airtight container up to 3 days or freeze up to 1 month.

Makes 30 servings

Per serving: 186 cal., 9 g total fat (4 g sat. fat), 9 mg chol., 122 mg sodium, 27 g carbo., 1 g fiber, 2 g pro.

Savory Nuts

To crush the thyme and rosemary, rub the dry herbs between your fingers right before tossing them into the recipe. Crushing releases essential oils in the herbs and intensifies their flavor.

Prep: 5 minutes   **Bake:** 12 minutes   **Cool:** 30 minutes   **Oven:** 350°F

4   cups assorted nuts (such as macadamia nuts, broken walnuts, and/or unblanched almonds)

¼   cup white wine Worcestershire sauce

2   Tbsp. olive oil

1   tsp. dried thyme, crushed

½   tsp. salt

½   tsp. dried rosemary, crushed

¼   tsp. cayenne pepper

1 Preheat oven to 350°F. Spread nuts in a 13×9×2-inch baking pan. Combine Worcestershire sauce, olive oil, thyme, salt, rosemary, and cayenne pepper; drizzle over nuts. Toss lightly to coat.

2 Bake, uncovered, for 12 to 15 minutes or until nuts are toasted, stirring occasionally. Spread mixture on a large piece of foil; cool for 30 minutes. Store in an airtight container up to 2 weeks.

Makes 16 servings

Per serving: 258 cal., 28 g total fat (4 g sat. fat), 0 mg chol., 192 mg sodium, 6 g carbo., 2 g fiber, 2 g pro.

German-Style Dip

This rich, robust dip owes much of its hearty flavor to caraway seeds, common in dishes from Germany, Austria, and Hungary, where they are loved for the nuttiness and licoricelike flavor.

Start to Finish: 25 minutes

½	cup finely chopped red onion
2	Tbsp. olive oil
2	8-oz. pkg. reduced-fat cream cheese (Neufchâtel), softened
1⅓	cups light sour cream
⅓	cup coarse-grain mustard
1	tsp. caraway seeds, crushed
	Dash black pepper
	Assorted dippers (such as peeled fresh baby carrots, cucumber spears, red cabbage leaves, roasted potato wedges, honey wheat braided twist pretzels, thinly sliced cooked ham wrapped around mini dill pickles, and/or cooked bratwurst slices)

1 In a saucepan cook onion in hot oil over medium-high heat about 4 minutes or until tender. Set aside to let cool for 15 minutes.

2 In a mixing bowl beat cream cheese with an electric mixer on medium speed until smooth. Gradually add sour cream, mustard, caraway seeds, and pepper; beat just until combined. Stir in cooled onion.

3 To serve, transfer dip to a serving dish. Serve with assorted dippers. Or cover and chill in the refrigerator up to 24 hours. Dip may be thicker after chilling. If necessary, stir in enough milk (1 to 2 tablespoons) to make a dipping consistency.

Makes 16 servings

Per serving: 83 cal., 7 g total fat (4 g sat. fat), 18 mg chol., 176 mg sodium, 3 g carbo., 0 g fiber, 2 g pro.

Fresh Summer Salsa

Fresh salsa, made from your own garden vegetables, surpasses any store-bought version.

Prep: 40 minutes   **Stand:** 30 minutes   **Chill:** 1 to 24 hours

¼   cup finely chopped red onion

¼   cup ice water

2   Tbsp. white wine vinegar

4   tomatillos, husked, rinsed, and finely chopped

¾   cup finely chopped yellow cherry tomatoes

⅔   cup finely chopped plum tomatoes (2)

1½   tsp. snipped fresh cilantro

1   medium fresh serrano chile pepper, seeded and finely chopped*

1   tsp. lime juice

Salt and black pepper

Tortilla chips

1 In a bowl combine onion, ice water, and vinegar; let stand for 30 minutes. Drain onion mixture; stir in tomatillos, cherry tomatoes, plum tomatoes, cilantro, serrano pepper, and lime juice. Season to taste with salt and black pepper. Cover and chill for 1 to 24 hours. Serve salsa with tortilla chips.

Makes about 3 cups (twelve ¼-cup servings)

Per serving: 79 cal., 4 g total fat (1 g sat. fat), 0 mg chol., 78 mg sodium, 11 g carbo., 1 g fiber, 1 g pro.

To tote: *Transport in an insulated cooler with ice packs. Pack chips in an airtight bag or container.*

***Note:** Because chile peppers contain volatile oils that can burn your skin and eyes, avoid direct contact with chiles as much as possible. When working with chile peppers, wear plastic or rubber gloves. If your bare hands do touch the chile peppers, wash your hands well with soap and water.*

Crab and Horseradish Havarti Dip

Havarti is a pale yellow semisoft Danish cheese. It boasts a mild, yet tangy flavor and a texture that makes this dip luxuriously creamy.

Prep: 15 minutes   **Bake:** 25 minutes   **Oven:** 350°F

- 2   8-oz. pkgs. cream cheese, softened
- 2½   cups shredded horseradish and chive Havarti cheese* (5 ounces)
- ⅔   cup sour cream
- ½   cup mayonnaise or salad dressing
- 2   cups cooked crabmeat or one 6-ounce can crabmeat, drained, flaked, and cartilage removed
- 2   cups shredded fresh baby spinach
- ⅔   cup thinly sliced green onions

  Flatbread, bagel chips, crostini, and/or toasted baguette-style French bread slices

1 Preheat oven to 350°F. In a large bowl combine cream cheese, 2 cups of the Havarti cheese, the sour cream, and mayonnaise; beat with an electric mixer on medium speed until well mixed. Gently stir in crabmeat and spinach.

2 Transfer mixture to a 2-quart baking dish. Bake about 25 minutes or until bubbly and heated through. Sprinkle with the remaining ½ cup Havarti cheese and the green onions. Serve with assorted breads.

Makes 24 (¼-cup) servings

Per serving: 175 cal., 16 g total fat (6 g sat. fat), 47 mg chol., 296 mg sodium, 1 g carbo., 0 g fiber, 7 g pro.

----

*Note: *If you can't find the horseradish and chive Havarti cheese, substitute 2½ cups shredded Havarti and add 2 tablespoons snipped fresh chives and 4 teaspoons prepared horseradish with the sour cream.*

Queso Fondue with Corn Bread Dippers

Of course you can use cubes of bread for dipping, but the corn bread dippers are perfect partners for this delicious fondue.

Prep: 45 minutes   **Bake:** 23 minutes   **Cool:** 10 minutes   **Oven:** 400°F

- 1   8.5-oz. pkg. corn muffin mix
- 3   cups shredded Monterey Jack cheese (12 ounces)
- 2   Tbsp. all-purpose flour
- ⅓   cup finely chopped onion
- 1   Tbsp. butter or margarine
- ¾   cup half-and-half or light cream
- 2   4-oz. cans diced green chile peppers, drained
- ⅓   cup chopped roasted red sweet peppers
- ⅓   cup finely chopped, peeled jicama

1 Preheat oven to 400°F. For the corn bread dippers, prepare corn muffin mix according to package directions. Spread batter in a greased 9×9×2-inch baking pan. Bake in a 400°F oven about 15 minutes or until golden. Cool bread in pan on a wire rack for 10 minutes. Remove bread from pan; cool completely on rack. Using a serrated knife, cut bread into ½-inch slices. Cut each slice into thirds. Place in a single layer on a large ungreased baking sheet. Bake for 8 to 10 minutes or until crisp and cut surfaces are golden, turning slices over after 5 minutes. Cool on a wire rack. Store in an airtight container for up to 2 days.

2 For fondue, toss together cheese and flour; set aside. In a medium saucepan cook onion in hot butter until tender; stir in half-and-half. Gradually add small amounts of the cheese mixture, stirring constantly over low heat until cheese is melted. Stir in chile peppers, roasted sweet peppers, and jicama; heat through. Transfer to a fondue pot; keep warm over a fondue burner.

Makes 48 servings

Per dipper with 2 teaspoons fondue: 60 cal., 4 g total fat (2 g sat. fat), 12 mg chol., 101 mg sodium, 5 g carbo., 0 g fiber, 2 g pro.

To tote: *Cover fondue tightly. Transport in an insulated carrier. Transfer to a fondue pot or slow cooker to serve. Transport dippers in an airtight container.*

White Bean Dip

It is highly unlikely that you will have any of this Italian-inspired dip left over—it's that good. If you do, use some as a sandwich spread with roast beef and tomatoes on a crisp baguette.

Prep: 20 minutes   **Chill:** 4 to 24 hours

¼ cup soft bread crumbs

2 Tbsp. dry white wine or water

1 19-oz. can cannellini beans (white kidney beans), rinsed and drained

¼ cup slivered almonds, toasted

2 to 3 cloves garlic, minced

2 Tbsp. lemon juice

2 Tbsp. olive oil

¼ tsp. salt

⅛ tsp. cayenne pepper

2 tsp. snipped fresh oregano or basil or ½ teaspoon dried oregano or basil, crushed

Fresh oregano or basil leaves (optional)

Toasted pita chips or assorted vegetable dippers (such as broccoli florets, carrot sticks, and/or yellow pepper strips)

1 In a bowl combine bread crumbs and wine; set aside to soak for 10 minutes.

2 Meanwhile, in a food processor or blender combine drained cannellini beans, almonds, garlic, lemon juice, olive oil, salt, and cayenne pepper. Cover and process or blend until almost smooth. Add bread crumb mixture; cover and process or blend until smooth. Transfer dip to a serving bowl. Stir in the 2 teaspoons oregano. Cover and chill in the refrigerator for 4 to 24 hours.

3 To serve, if desired, garnish dip with fresh oregano leaves. Serve with toasted pita chips and/or vegetable dippers.

Makes 16 servings

Per serving: 50 cal., 3 g total fat (0 g sat. fat), 0 mg chol., 93 mg sodium, 6 g carbo., 2 g fiber, 2 g pro.

Supreme Pizza Fondue

Italian sausage is available in two versions—hot, which is spiced up with hot peppers, and mild, which is heat-free. The mild variety is sometimes called sweet Italian sausage.

Start to Finish: 25 minutes

- 4   oz. bulk Italian sausage
- ⅓   cup finely chopped onion
- 1   clove garlic, minced
- 1   26-oz. jar spaghetti sauce
- 1   cup chopped fresh mushrooms
- ⅔   cup chopped pepperoni or Canadian-style bacon
- 1   tsp. dried basil or oregano, crushed
- ½   cup chopped pitted ripe olives (optional)
- ¼   cup finely chopped green sweet pepper (optional)

   Assorted dippers (such as Italian bread cubes, cooked tortellini, and/or mozzarella or provolone cheese cubes)

1 In a skillet cook the sausage, onion, and garlic over medium-high heat until meat is brown. Drain off fat.

2 Add spaghetti sauce, mushrooms, pepperoni, and basil. Heat to boiling; reduce heat. Simmer, covered, for 10 minutes. If desired, stir in ripe olives and sweet pepper. Simmer, covered, about 5 minutes more or until sweet pepper is tender.

3 To serve, transfer sausage mixture to a fondue pot; keep warm over a fondue burner. Serve with assorted dippers.

Makes 16 servings

Per serving: 59 cal., 4 g total fat (2 g sat. fat), 10 mg chol., 296 mg sodium, 3 g carbo., 1 g fiber, 3 g pro.

Crab-Caper Dip

This elegant dip is perfect for special occasions. A hollowed-out round bread loaf creates an edible serving container.

Prep: 25 minutes   **Bake:** 55 minutes   **Oven:** 350°F

1   8- to 10-inch round bread loaf, unsliced

2   cups chopped onions

2   cups light mayonnaise dressing

8   oz. reduced-fat Swiss cheese, finely chopped*

1   cup cooked lump crabmeat or one 6-oz. can crabmeat, drained and flaked

¼   cup capers, drained

Assorted vegetable dippers

1 Cut the top off the bread loaf and hollow out the inside. Place top and hollow bread loaf in an airtight container. Set aside.

2 Preheat oven to 350°F. In a medium saucepan cook onions, covered, in a small amount of boiling water for 5 minutes; drain well. In a large bowl stir together the cooked onions, mayonnaise dressing, Swiss cheese, crabmeat, and capers.

3 Spoon crab mixture into a 1½-quart casserole. Bake, covered, about 55 minutes or until heated through. Serve with vegetable dippers.

Makes 40 (2 tablespoon) servings

Per serving: 65 cal., 4 g total fat (1 g sat. fat), 10 mg chol., 132 mg sodium, 4 g carbo., 1 g fiber, 3 g pro.

To tote: *Transport dip in an insulated carrier. Transport bread loaf in an airtight container. To serve, spoon dip into hollowed-out bread loaf.*

---

*Note: *Reduced-fat cheese is preferable to regular-fat Swiss in this recipe because the reduced-fat cheese doesn't break down as easily during the long baking.*

Spicy Spinach-Stuffed Mushrooms

For a beautiful buffet presentation—and to keep mushrooms from sliding on the serving platter— place the caps on a bed of shredded spinach or warmed rock salt.

Prep: 30 minutes   **Bake:** 10 minutes   **Oven:** 425°F

24	large fresh mushrooms, 1½ to 2 inches in diameter
2	Tbsp. olive oil
	Salt
	Ground black pepper
8	oz. spicy bulk Italian sausage
¼	cup finely chopped onion
¼	cup finely chopped red sweet pepper
2	cloves garlic, minced
1	cup fresh spinach, chopped
¼	cup finely shredded Parmesan cheese
¼	cup fine dry bread crumbs

1 Preheat oven to 425°F. Rinse and drain mushrooms. Remove stems and chop; set aside. Brush mushroom caps with olive oil. Sprinkle with salt and black pepper. Set aside.

2 In a skillet cook chopped stems, sausage, onion, sweet pepper, and garlic over medium heat until sausage is brown. Stir in spinach until wilted. Stir in Parmesan cheese and bread crumbs. Remove from heat. Spoon sausage mixture into mushroom caps. Place on a greased baking sheet.

3 Bake, uncovered, for 10 to 12 minutes or until stuffing is brown and mushrooms are tender.

Makes 24 servings

Per serving: 53 cal., 4 g total fat (2 g sat. fat), 7 mg chol., 179 mg sodium, 2 g carbo., 0 g fiber, 3 g pro.

Easy Vegetable Dip

When you have an after-work party to attend, blend the ingredients together while you're home for lunch, cover and refrigerate the dip, then pick it up on your way to the party.

Prep: 15 minutes   **Chill:** 2 to 48 hours

1   cup mayonnaise or salad dressing

1   8-oz. carton sour cream

6   green onions, cut into 3-inch pieces

6   sprigs fresh parsley, stems removed

¼   tsp. garlic powder

Assorted vegetable dippers (such as sweet red pepper, broccoli florets, cauliflower florets, or carrot sticks) and/or crackers

1 In a food processor or blender combine mayonnaise, sour cream, green onions, parsley, and garlic powder. Cover and process or blend until smooth. Cover and chill for 2 to 48 hours. Serve with vegetable dippers.

Makes 2¼ cups (eighteen 2-tablespoon servings)

Per serving: 137 cal., 13 g total fat (3 g sat. fat), 13 mg chol., 94 mg sodium, 6 g carbo., 2 g fiber, 2 g pro.

- -

To tote: *Transport dip and vegetable dippers in an insulated cooler with ice packs. Pack crackers in an airtight bag or container.*

Shrimp with Mustard Cream Sauce

Oh-so-elegant describes these tasty shrimp. If you're short on time, omit the snow peas.

Prep: 25 minutes   **Chill:** 2 to 24 hours

1½	lb. fresh or frozen medium shrimp in shells, peeled and deveined (leave tails intact, if desired)
36	snow peas
1	8-oz. carton sour cream
2	Tbsp. Dijon-style mustard
2	tsp. milk
½	tsp. black pepper
1	Tbsp. capers, drained

1 Thaw shrimp, if frozen. In a large saucepan cook shrimp and snow peas, uncovered, in boiling lightly salted water about 2 minutes or until shrimp turn opaque; drain. Rinse under cold running water; drain again. Cool. Wrap a snow pea around each shrimp. Secure with a wooden toothpick. Cover and chill for 2 to 24 hours.

2 For sauce, in a small bowl stir together sour cream, mustard, milk, and pepper. Cover and chill for 2 to 24 hours.

3 To serve, sprinkle sauce with capers. Serve shrimp with sauce.

Makes 12 servings

Per serving: 109 cal., 5 g total fat (3 g sat. fat), 95 mg chol., 131 mg sodium, 2 g carbo., 0 g fiber, 12 g pro.

To tote: *Transport shrimp and sauce in an insulated cooler with ice packs.*

Tequila Shrimp with Dried-Tomato Mayo

Dunk marinated shrimp in a garlic-and-tomato mayonnaise for an unforgettable appetizer. Use precooked shrimp to make this recipe even easier.

Prep: 30 minutes   **Marinate:** 2 hours   **Chill:** 2 hours

- 1   lb. fresh or frozen large shrimp in shells, peeled and deveined (leave tails intact, if desired)
- ½   cup tequila
- ¼   cup finely chopped onion
- ¼   cup lime juice
- 2   Tbsp. snipped fresh cilantro or parsley
- 2   Tbsp. olive oil
- ½   cup dried tomatoes (not oil-packed)
- 1   cup mayonnaise or salad dressing
- 1   Tbsp. snipped fresh cilantro or parsley
- 1   Tbsp. milk
- 1   tsp. bottled minced garlic
- ⅛   tsp. salt
       Crushed ice
       Lime wedges

1 Thaw shrimp, if frozen. In a large saucepan cook shrimp, uncovered, in boiling lightly salted water for 2 to 3 minutes or until shrimp turn opaque; drain. Rinse under cold running water; drain again. Place shrimp in a heavy plastic bag set in a shallow dish.

2 For marinade, in a bowl combine tequila, onion, lime juice, the 2 tablespoons cilantro, and olive oil. Pour marinade over shrimp; seal bag. Marinate in the refrigerator for 2 hours, turning bag occasionally.

3 For mayonnaise mixture, in a small bowl cover dried tomatoes with boiling water; let stand for 5 minutes. Drain well. Finely chop tomatoes. In a small bowl combine chopped tomatoes, mayonnaise, the 1 tablespoon cilantro, milk, garlic, and salt. Transfer to a serving bowl. Cover and chill about 2 hours or until ready to serve.

4 To serve, drain shrimp, discarding marinade. Transfer to serving bowl. Place serving bowl in a larger bowl filled with crushed ice. Serve with mayonnaise mixture and lime wedges.

Makes 10 servings

Per serving: 220 cal., 19 g total fat (3 g sat. fat), 60 mg chol., 258 mg sodium, 3 g carbo., 0 g fiber, 7 g pro.

To tote: *Transport shrimp, mayonnaise mixture, and lime wedges in an insulated cooler with ice packs.*

Note: *For a nonalcoholic version, omit the tequila from the marinade.*

Double-Quick Shrimp Cocktail

Talk about a triple play! This starter pleases shrimp lovers and dazzles those who adore a creamy dip as well as the piquant red classic.

Start to Finish: 15 minutes

- 1 8-oz. carton sour cream
- ¼ cup prepared horseradish
- 2 Tbsp. snipped chives or thinly sliced green onion tops
- 1 Tbsp. lemon juice
- 1 12-oz. jar seafood cocktail sauce or chili sauce
- 1½ lb. frozen peeled and cooked shrimp with tails, thawed (60 to 75)

  Chives and/or lemon slices or wedges

1 In a bowl combine sour cream, horseradish, snipped chives, and lemon juice. If desired, cover and chill in the refrigerator up to 4 hours before serving.

2 To serve, transfer sour cream mixture to a shallow serving dish. Spoon seafood cocktail sauce into another serving dish. Place both serving dishes on a large serving platter. Arrange shrimp around dishes. Garnish with chives and/or lemon slices or wedges.

Makes 40 servings

Per serving: 37 cal., 1 g total fat (1 g sat. fat), 36 mg chol., 119 mg sodium, 2 g carbo., 0 g fiber, 4 g pro.

Spicy Cajun Shrimp

There are many Cajun seasonings on the market. Most of these blends share common ingredients: garlic, onion, chiles, pepper, mustard, and celery seeds.

Start to Finish: 25 minutes

- 2 lb. fresh or frozen large shrimp in shells
- 1 cup mayonnaise or salad dressing
- ¼ cup tomato paste
- 2 Tbsp. lemon juice
- 2 clove garlic, minced
- ¼ cup butter or margarine, melted
- 2 Tbsp. Cajun seasoning

1 Thaw shrimp, if frozen. Peel and devein shrimp, leaving tails intact if desired. Rinse shrimp; pat dry with paper towels; set aside.

2 For sauce, in a bowl combine mayonnaise, tomato paste, lemon juice, and garlic. Cover and chill in the refrigerator until ready to serve.

3 Preheat broiler. Brush both sides of each shrimp with melted butter. Sprinkle both sides of each shrimp with Cajun seasoning. Place shrimp on the unheated rack of a broiler pan.

4 Broil 4 to 5 inches from the heat for 2 minutes. Turn shrimp; broil for 1 to 2 minutes more or until shrimp are opaque. Serve shrimp with sauce.

Makes 32 servings

Per serving: 181 cal., 15 g total fat (3 g sat. fat), 83 mg chol., 264 mg sodium, 2 g carbo., 0 g fiber, 9 g pro.

Buffalo-Style Chicken Fingers

This version of Buffalo wings is the healthful way to go. A serving of this recipe contains half the calories and two-thirds less fat than the same serving size of traditional Buffalo wings.

Prep: 25 minutes   **Bake:** 18 minutes per batch   **Oven:** 425°F

- 4   cups crushed cornflakes
- ¼   cup finely snipped parsley
- 1   tsp. salt
- 2   lb. skinless, boneless chicken breast halves
- ⅔   cup bottled blue cheese salad dressing
- 4   tsp. water
- 2   to 4 tsp. bottled hot pepper sauce
-      Celery sticks
-      Bottled blue cheese salad dressing

1 Preheat oven to 425°F. In a shallow bowl or pie plate combine crushed cornflakes, parsley, and salt. Cut chicken breasts into strips about ¾ inch wide and 3 inches long.

2 In a bowl combine the ⅔ cup blue cheese salad dressing, the water, and hot pepper sauce. Add chicken; stir to coat. Roll chicken pieces individually in crumb mixture to coat.

3 Place chicken strips in a single layer in two lightly greased 15×10×1-inch baking pans. Bake, one pan at a time, for 18 to 20 minutes or until chicken is no longer pink and crumbs are golden.

4 To serve, transfer chicken to a serving platter. Serve warm with celery sticks and additional blue cheese dressing for dipping.

Makes 24 servings

Per serving: 184 cal., 12 g total fat (2 g sat. fat), 26 mg chol., 408 mg sodium, 9 g carbo., 0 g fiber, 11 g pro.

Thai Chicken Wings with Peanut Sauce

When peeling ginger, remove only the skin. The flesh immediately below the surface is most flavorful. For easy grating, freeze ginger for 15 minutes.

Prep: 25 minutes   **Bake:** 20 minutes   **Oven:** 400°F

2¼ lb. chicken wing drummettes (about 20)
½ cup salsa
2 Tbsp. creamy peanut butter
1 Tbsp. lime juice
2 tsp. soy sauce
2 tsp. grated fresh ginger
¼ cup sugar
¼ cup creamy peanut butter
3 Tbsp. soy sauce
3 Tbsp. water
2 cloves garlic, minced
Shredded bok choy (optional)
Lime wedges (optional)

1 Preheat oven to 400°F. Place drummettes in a large bowl. Combine salsa, the 2 tablespoons peanut butter, the lime juice, the 2 teaspoons soy sauce, and ginger. Pour over drummettes, tossing to coat.

2 Arrange drummettes in a single layer in a baking pan or roasting pan lined with foil. Bake, uncovered, about 20 minutes or until tender and no longer pink.

3 Meanwhile, for the peanut sauce, in a saucepan combine sugar, the ¼ cup peanut butter, the 3 tablespoons soy sauce, the water, and garlic. Cook and stir over medium-low heat until sugar is dissolved and mixture is smooth.

4 To serve, transfer warm drummettes to a serving platter and pour peanut sauce into a serving bowl. Serve sauce with drummettes (sauce will thicken as it stands). If desired, garnish with shredded bok choy and lime wedges.

Makes 12 servings

Per serving: 189 cal., 13 g total fat (3 g sat. fat), 58 mg chol., 392 mg sodium, 6 g carbo., 1 g fiber, 12 g pro.

Sweet and Sour Chicken Wings

Sweetly glazed with pineapple juice, ketchup, and soy sauce, these are a can't-miss choice for potlucks.

Prep: 20 minutes   **Bake:** 30 minutes   **Oven:** 350°F

2½ lb. chicken wings (12 to 15)

½ cup all-purpose flour

½ tsp. lemon-pepper seasoning

¼ tsp. garlic salt

3 Tbsp. vegetable oil

⅔ cup sugar

½ cup white wine vinegar or rice vinegar

¼ cup unsweetened pineapple juice

¼ cup ketchup

1 tsp. soy sauce

Green onions (optional)

1 Cut off and discard tips of chicken wings. Cut wings at joints to form 24 to 30 pieces.

2 In a shallow dish combine flour, lemon-pepper seasoning, and garlic salt. Coat each chicken piece with the flour mixture.

3 Heat oil in an extra-large skillet. Add coated chicken pieces to skillet. Cook, uncovered, until brown, turning occasionally. Remove chicken pieces from skillet and arrange in a 3-quart rectangular baking dish.

4 In a medium saucepan whisk together sugar, vinegar, pineapple juice, ketchup, and soy sauce. Bring to boiling, stirring to dissolve sugar; pour over chicken. Bake, uncovered, in a 350°F oven about 30 minutes or until chicken is tender and no longer pink, turning pieces over after 15 minutes. If desired, garnish with green onions.

Makes 24 to 30 pieces

Per piece: 153 cal., 9 g total fat (2 g sat. fat), 36 mg chol., 108 mg sodium, 9 g carbo., 0 g fiber, 9 g pro.

To tote: *Cover tightly. Transport chicken wings and, if desired, green onions in an insulated carrier.*

Plum-Good Sausage and Meatballs

If you are lucky enough to have any party leftovers, serve these saucy meatballs and sausages over hot cooked rice for a family-friendly main dish.

Prep: 10 minutes   **Cook:** 5 hours (low) or 2½ hours (high)

- 2   10-oz. or 12-oz. jars plum jam or preserves
- 2   18-oz. bottles barbecue sauce
- 2   16-oz. pkg. cooked jalapeño smoked sausage or smoked sausage, sliced into bite-size pieces
- 2   16-oz. to 18-oz. pkg. Italian-style or regular frozen cooked meatballs, thawed

1 In a 5- or 6-quart slow cooker combine jam, barbecue sauce, sausage, and thawed meatballs.

2 Cover and cook on low-heat setting for 5 to 6 hours or on high-heat setting for 2½ to 3 hours.

3 Serve immediately or keep warm on warm setting or low-heat setting for up to 2 hours. Stir occasionally.

Makes 32 servings

Per serving: 267 cal., 16 g total fat (6 g sat. fat), 38 mg chol., 898 mg sodium, 19 g carbo., 2 g fiber, 12 g pro.

Sweet, Hot, and Sour Meatballs

If kids are on the guest list, apple juice is a fine substitute for the whiskey in these tasty sausage and beef meatballs.

Prep: 20 minutes   **Bake:** 30 minutes   **Oven:** 375°F

½   cup refrigerated or frozen egg product, thawed

½   cup fine dry bread crumbs

½   cup finely chopped onion

¼   cup milk

½   tsp. salt

½   tsp. black pepper

1   lb. bulk pork sausage

1   lb. ground beef

¾   cup apple jelly

⅓   cup spicy brown mustard

⅓   cup whiskey or apple juice

1½ tsp. Worcestershire sauce

Few dashes bottled hot pepper sauce

1 In a large bowl combine egg product, bread crumbs, onion, milk, salt, and pepper. Add sausage and beef; mix well. Shape into 48 meatballs. Place meatballs in a shallow baking pan. Bake, uncovered, in a 375°F oven about 30 minutes or until done (160°F). Remove from oven; drain.

2 Meanwhile, in a large saucepan stir together jelly, mustard, whiskey, Worcestershire sauce, and bottled hot pepper sauce. Heat and stir until jelly melts and mixture bubbles. Add meatballs, stirring gently to coat. Cook for 3 to 5 minutes or until sauce thickens slightly and meatballs are coated.

Makes 24 servings (48 meatballs)

Per serving: 154 cal., 8 g total fat (3 g sat. fat), 23 mg chol., 232 mg sodium, 9 g carbo., 0 g fiber, 7 g pro.

- -

To tote: *Transfer meatballs and sauce to a serving dish; cover tightly. Transport in an insulated carrier.*

Sweet and Sassy Meatballs

These roly-poly orbs of goodness are so easy that a child can make them. Invite one of the kids to join you in the kitchen for some fun.

Start to Finish: 20 minutes

- 1 18-oz. bottle barbecue sauce
- 1 16-oz. bottle jellied cranberry sauce
- 2 1-lb. pkg. (64 total) frozen cooked meatballs, thawed

1 For sauce, in a skillet combine barbecue sauce and cranberry sauce. Cook over medium heat until cranberry sauce is melted, stirring occasionally.

2 Add meatballs to sauce. Cook, uncovered, for 10 minutes or until meatballs are heated through, stirring occasionally.

3 To serve, transfer to a chafing dish or slow cooker; keep warm.

Makes 64 servings

Per serving: 60 cal., 4 g total fat (2 g sat. fat), 5 mg chol., 177 mg sodium, 5 g carbo., 1 g fiber, 2 g pro.

Date-Sausage Bites

Rarely you'll happen across a food pairing that's a match made in heaven. Dates and sausages are just such a marriage of wonderful flavors: sweetness from the dates and savory saltiness from the sausage.

Prep: 25 minutes   **Bake:** 20 minutes per batch   **Oven:** 400°F

- 1   17.3-oz. pkg. (2 sheets) frozen puff pastry, thawed
- 12   oz. maple-flavored bulk pork sausage
- 1   cup chopped pitted dates
- 1   tsp. garlic powder
- ½   tsp. dried sage or oregano, crushed
- ¼   tsp. crushed red pepper
- ¼   tsp. black pepper

1 Preheat oven to 400°F. Carefully unfold the pastry. Cut along folds, making 6 rectangles; set aside.

2 For filling, in a bowl combine sausage, dates, garlic powder, sage, red pepper, and black pepper. Spread abut ¼ cup filling lengthwise down half of each pastry rectangle to within ½ inch of one long edge. Fold the other long side of pastry over meat mixture; pinch edges to seal. Cut filled pastries into 1-inch pieces. Place the pieces, pastry sides down, on two ungreased 15×10×1-inch baking pans.

3 Bake, one pan at a time, about 20 minutes or until golden brown. Serve warm.

Makes 24 servings

Per serving: 75 cal., 5 g total fat (1 g sat. fat), 4 mg chol., 76 mg sodium, 6 g carbo., 0 g fiber, 1 g pro.

Mushroom-Bacon Turnovers

The meaty flesh of shiitake [shee-TAH-kay] mushrooms is gutsy and robust almost like steak in flavor. The stems, however, are tough, so use only the caps in this recipe.

Prep: 30 minutes **Bake:** 14 minutes per batch **Oven:** 350°F

- ¼ cup butter or margarine
- 4 cups chopped fresh brown or button mushrooms
- 2 cups chopped fresh shiitake mushrooms (caps only)
- ⅔ cup finely chopped red onion
- ⅓ cup whipping cream
- 6 slices bacon, crisp-cooked, drained, and crumbled
- 2 Tbsp. snipped fresh thyme
- 2 Tbsp. snipped fresh basil
- 2 17.3-oz. pkg. (16 total) refrigerated large biscuits
- 2 eggs

1 Preheat oven to 350°F. For filling, in a skillet melt butter over medium heat. Add mushrooms and onion. Cook about 5 minutes or until mushrooms are tender, stirring occasionally. Stir in whipping cream. Simmer, uncovered, for 2 minutes more. Remove skillet from heat. Stir in bacon, thyme, and basil.

2 Using your fingers, separate each biscuit in half so you have 32 biscuit rounds. On a lightly floured surface, use the palm of your hand to flatten each biscuit round to a 3-inch circle. Place about 2 teaspoons of the filling onto one half of each circle of dough. Fold dough over filling; seal edges by pressing them together firmly with tines of a fork. Place filled turnovers on two ungreased baking sheets.

3 In a bowl beat eggs with a whisk; brush egg over turnovers. Bake, one sheet at a time, for 14 to 17 minutes or until turnovers are golden. Serve warm.

Makes 32 servings

Per serving: 139 cal., 8 g total fat (3 g sat. fat), 22 mg chol., 310 mg sodium, 13 g carbo., 1 g fiber, 3 g pro.

Tortellini, Olive, and Cheese Kabobs

If you like, you can serve this recipe in a bowl rather than as kabobs. Have plenty of toothpicks available for spearing.

Prep: 25 minutes   **Chill:** 3 to 4 hours

⅔ cup bottled oil-and-vinegar salad dressing

3 Tbsp. purchased basil pesto

2 cups frozen cheese-filled tortellini

8 oz. cheddar cheese and/or Monterey Jack cheese with jalapeño peppers, cut into ½- to ¾-inch cubes

30 assorted pitted olives (such as ripe or kalamata olives or pimiento-stuffed or onion-stuffed green olives)

30 red or green pickled jalapeño peppers

1 For marinade, in a medium bowl combine salad dressing and pesto; set aside.

2 Meanwhile, cook tortellini according to package directions; drain. Rinse with cold water; drain again.

3 On 6-inch picks or skewers, alternately thread the cooked tortellini, cheese cubes, olives, and pickled peppers. Place kabobs in a 13×9×2-inch baking dish. Brush with marinade. Cover and chill for 3 to 4 hours.

Makes 30 kabobs (15 servings)

Per serving: 74 cal., 4 g total fat (2 g sat. fat), 9 mg chol., 293 mg sodium, 5 g carbo., 1 g fiber, 3 g pro.

To tote: *Transport in an insulated cooler with ice packs.*

Chicken and Orzo Casserole, page 66

Chapter 2

Favorite Poultry Dishes

Curried Pasta and Chicken Salad

Widely used in Indian cooking, curry powder is a mixture of up to 20 spices. Buy it in small quantities as it keeps its flavor for only 2 months.

Prep: 25 minutes   **Chill:** 4 to 24 hours

- 3 cups (12 oz.) dried radiatore or rotini pasta
- 3 cups (about 15 oz.) cubed cooked chicken
- 2¼ cups seedless green grapes, halved
- 2¼ cups cubed cantaloupe
- 1¼ cups sliced celery
- ¾ cup sliced green onions
- ¼ cup chutney
- 1½ cups plain low-fat yogurt
- 2¼ tsp. curry powder
- ½ tsp. salt
- Milk (optional)

1 Cook pasta according to package directions. Drain; rinse with cold water. Drain again.

2 In a bowl combine pasta, chicken, grapes, cantaloupe, celery, and green onion.

3 For dressing, cut up any large pieces in chutney. In a bowl stir together chutney, yogurt, curry powder, and salt. Pour dressing over pasta mixture. Toss to coat. Cover and chill for 4 to 24 hours.

4 Before serving, if necessary, stir in milk, 1 tablespoon at a time, until salad is creamy.

Makes 9 servings

Per serving: 314 cal., 5 g total fat (2 g sat. fat), 44 mg chol., 204 mg sodium, 46 g carbo., 3 g fiber, 21 g pro.

Chinese-Style Pasta Salad

Pasta steps in for steamed rice in this Asian-inspired salad. Be sure to purchase an Asian salad dressing to stay true to the salad's intended flavor.

Prep: 25 minutes   **Chill:** 4 to 24 hours

1	16-oz. pkg. dried fettuccine or linguine
4	cups chopped cooked chicken*
1½	cups thinly bias-sliced celery
½	cup sliced green onions
¼	cup snipped fresh cilantro or parsley
1	8-oz. bottle Asian vinaigrette salad dressing
2	tsp. sesame seeds, toasted

1 Cook fettuccine according to package directions; drain. Rinse with cold water; drain again. Transfer fettuccine to a very large bowl. Stir in chicken, celery, green onions, and cilantro. Pour dressing over all; toss to coat well. Cover and chill for 4 to 24 hours. Just before serving, sprinkle with sesame seeds.

Makes 8 servings

Per serving: 399 cal., 9 g total fat (2 g sat. fat), 62 mg chol., 754 mg sodium, 48 g carbo., 2 g fiber, 29 g pro.

To tote: *Transport salad and sesame seeds in an insulated cooler with ice packs.*

*Note: *About 1½ pounds boneless chicken breasts will yield 4 cups chopped cooked chicken.*

Hot Chicken Salad

This hot chicken salad derives its creaminess from sour cream, mozzarella cheese, and cream of chicken soup. Serve with slices of toasted French bread.

Prep: 30 minutes   **Bake:** 30 minutes   **Stand:** 10 minutes   **Oven:** 400°F

- 1 cup coarsely crushed potato chips
- ⅔ cup finely chopped almonds
- 6 cups cubed cooked chicken*
- 3 cups chopped celery
- 1 10.75-oz. can condensed cream of chicken soup
- 2 cups (8 oz.) shredded mozzarella cheese
- 2 8-oz. cartons sour cream or plain yogurt
- ¼ cup chopped onion
- 1 tsp. dried thyme or basil, crushed
- 4 hard-cooked eggs, chopped

1 Preheat oven to 400°F. In a small bowl combine potato chips and almonds; set aside. In a very large bowl combine chicken, celery, soup, cheese, sour cream, onion, and thyme. Gently fold in hard-cooked eggs. Transfer to a 3-quart rectangular baking dish. Sprinkle with potato chip mixture.

2 Bake, uncovered, for 30 to 35 minutes or until heated through. Let stand for 10 minutes before serving (if toting, see note).

Makes 12 servings

Per serving: 398 cal., 25 g total fat (10 g sat. fat), 168 mg chol., 437 mg sodium, 9 g carbo., 2 g fiber, 33 g pro.

To tote: *Do not let stand after baking. Cover tightly. Transport in an insulated carrier.*

*Note: *About 2¼ pounds boneless chicken breasts will yield 6 cups chopped cooked chicken.*

Smoked Chicken Strata

Call on strata—the classic brunch dish—for special holiday mornings or for evenings when breakfast for supper sounds especially good.

Prep: 25 minutes   **Chill:** 2 to 24 hours   **Bake:** 25 minutes   **Stand:** 10 minutes   **Oven:** 325°F

1	Tbsp. vegetable oil
2	cups cut-up fresh asparagus or chopped fresh broccoli
1½	cups sliced fresh mushrooms
½	cup chopped red or yellow sweet pepper
	Nonstick cooking spray
3	whole grain English muffins, torn or cut into bite-size pieces
2	cups (about 10 oz.) shredded smoked chicken or cooked chicken breast
¾	cup (3 oz.) shredded Swiss cheese
4	eggs, beaten
1	cup milk
⅛	tsp. black pepper

1 In a large nonstick skillet heat oil over medium-high heat. Add asparagus, mushrooms, and sweet pepper; cook and stir about 3 minutes or just until vegetables are crisp-tender.

2 Lightly coat six 12-ounce casseroles with cooking spray. Divide half of the English muffin pieces among the dishes. Top with chicken, asparagus mixture, and two-thirds of the cheese. Top with the remaining English muffin pieces.

3 In a bowl whisk together eggs, milk, and black pepper. Pour egg mixture evenly over the layers in dishes. Using the back of a large spoon, press muffin pieces down to moisten. Sprinkle with the remaining cheese. Cover and chill for 2 to 24 hours.

4 Preheat oven to 325°F. Bake, uncovered, for 25 to 30 minutes or until a knife inserted in centers comes out clean. Let stand for 10 minutes before serving.

Makes 6 servings

Per serving: 277 cal., 12 g total fat (4 g sat. fat), 178 mg chol., 746 mg sodium, 21 g carbo., 4 g fiber, 23 g pro.

Chicken Alfredo and Rice Casserole

To prepare two cups of soft bread crumbs, tear three to four slices of day-old bread in small pieces. Place in a food processor or blender and pulse until light, fluffy crumbs form.

Prep: 25 minutes   **Bake:** 50 minutes   **Stand:** 5 minutes   **Oven:** 350°F

2   10-oz. containers refrigerated light Alfredo pasta sauce

1   cup milk

5   cups cooked white rice or wild rice

4   cups (about 1¼ lb.) cubed cooked chicken

2   cups frozen peas

⅔   cup chopped bottled roasted red sweet peppers

½   cup slivered almonds, toasted (optional)

2   Tbsp. snipped fresh basil

2   cups soft bread crumbs

2   Tbsp. butter, melted

1 Preheat oven to 350°F. In a large bowl combine pasta sauce and milk. Stir in rice, chicken, peas, roasted red peppers, almonds (if using), and basil. Transfer to a 3-quart casserole. Cover with foil.

2 Bake for 30 minutes. Uncover and stir. In a bowl combine bread crumbs and melted butter; sprinkle on top of pasta mixture. Bake, uncovered, for 20 to 25 minutes more or until heated through and crumbs are golden. Let stand for 5 minutes before serving.

Makes 8 servings

Per serving: 456 cal., 16 g total fat (8 g sat. fat), 97 mg chol., 672 mg sodium, 45 g carbo., 3 g fiber, 32 g pro.

Hot and Cheesy Chicken Casserole

Here's what every busy mom is looking for—nearly every food group in one quick-fix dish. To complete the food pyramid, serve this colorful casserole with a spinach-orange salad.

Prep: 35 minutes **Bake:** 35 minutes **Oven:** 350°F

3	cups (about 15 oz.) chopped cooked chicken
1	14-oz. pkg. frozen broccoli florets
2	cups cooked rice
1½	cups frozen peas
1	10.75-oz. can condensed cream of chicken soup
1	10.75-oz. can condensed fiesta nacho cheese soup
1	10-oz. can diced tomatoes and green chilies, undrained
½	cup milk
½	tsp. crushed red pepper (optional)
½	cup (2 oz.) shredded cheddar cheese
½	cup (2 oz.) shredded mozzarella cheese
1	cup crushed rich round crackers

1 Preheat oven to 350°F. Place chicken in a 3-quart rectangular baking dish. In a large bowl combine broccoli, rice, and peas. Spread mixture over chicken.

2 In a bowl combine cream of chicken soup, nacho cheese soup, undrained tomatoes, milk, and, if desired, crushed red pepper. Stir in half of the cheddar cheese and half of the mozzarella cheese. Pour mixture over broccoli mixture in baking dish. Sprinkle crushed crackers evenly over all. Top with the remaining cheddar cheese and the remaining mozzarella cheese.

3 Bake, uncovered, 35 to 40 minutes or until topping is golden.

Makes 8 to 10 servings

Per serving: 354 cal., 15 g total fat (6 g sat. fat), 65 mg chol., 886 mg sodium, 29 g carbo., 4 g fiber, 26 g pro.

Lazy Paella

Preparing the Spanish specialty paella [pi-AY-yuh] is normally a long and involved process. This recipe, however, yields scrumptious results with a fraction of the effort.

Prep: 25 minutes **Bake:** 45 minutes **Stand:** 10 minutes **Oven:** 350°F

Nonstick cooking spray
¼ cup vegetable oil
5 to 6 lb. chicken thighs, skinned
2 14-oz. cans chicken broth
2 cups long grain rice
2 cups frozen peas, thawed
2 cups cooked, peeled, and deveined shrimp
2 4-oz. cans (drained weight) sliced mushrooms, drained
¼ cup dry onion soup mix
Salt
Black pepper
Paprika

1 Preheat oven to 350°F. Lightly coat two 3-quart rectangular baking dishes with cooking spray; set aside. In a large skillet heat half of the oil over medium heat. Add half of the chicken; cook in hot oil, turning to brown evenly. Remove chicken from skillet; set aside. Repeat with remaining chicken and oil.

2 In a large bowl combine broth, uncooked rice, peas, shrimp, mushrooms, and dry soup mix. Divide mixture between prepared baking dishes. Arrange chicken on top of rice mixture. Sprinkle chicken lightly with salt, pepper, and paprika. Cover baking dishes tightly with foil.

3 Bake about 45 minutes or until chicken is no longer pink (180°F). Let stand, covered, for 10 minutes before serving.

Makes 8 to 12 servings

Per serving: 500 cal., 12 g total fat (2 g sat. fat), 212 mg chol., 1,101 mg sodium, 47 g carbo., 3 g fiber, 49 g pro.

Spicy Chicken and Rice Bake

Invite healthful black beans to the table. These velvet-texture black beauties are inexpensive, rich in cholesterol-reducing fiber, and packed with disease-fighting antioxidants.

Prep: 25 minutes   **Bake:** 55 minutes   **Oven:** 375°F

2	Tbsp. vegetable oil
1	cup chopped onion
1	cup chopped green sweet pepper
4	cloves garlic, minced
2	15-oz. cans black beans, rinsed and drained
2	14.5-oz. cans diced tomatoes, undrained
2	cups tomato juice
2	cups frozen whole kernel corn
1⅓	cups long grain rice
2	tsp. chili powder
1	tsp. salt
¼	to ½ tsp. cayenne pepper
6	lb. meaty chicken pieces (small breast halves, thighs, and drumsticks), skinned
	Salt
	Black pepper
	Paprika

1 Preheat oven to 375°F. In a large saucepan heat oil over medium heat. Add onion, sweet pepper, and garlic; cook and stir until vegetables are tender. Stir in beans, undrained tomatoes, tomato juice, corn, uncooked rice, chili powder, salt, and cayenne pepper. Bring to boiling. Divide rice mixture between two 3-quart rectangular baking dishes.

2 Arrange chicken pieces on top of the rice mixture. Sprinkle chicken lightly with salt, black pepper, and paprika. Cover baking dishes tightly with foil.

3 Bake for 55 to 60 minutes or until chicken is no longer pink (170°F for breasts; 180°F for thighs and drumsticks) and rice is tender.

Makes 12 servings

Per serving: 446 cal., 15 g total fat (4 g sat. fat), 104 mg chol., 854 mg sodium, 39 g carbo., 6 g fiber, 40 g pro.

Chicken and Noodles with Vegetables

Warm, tender, and fragrant, this dish is the quintessential comfort food to bring the family to the table on a chilly winter evening.

Prep: 30 minutes   **Cook:** 8 hours (low) or 4 hours (high)

- 3 cups sliced carrot
- 2¼ cups chopped onion
- 1½ cups sliced celery
- 1 bay leaf
- 6 medium (about 3¾ lb. total) chicken legs (drumstick-thigh portion), skinned
- 3 10.75-ounce cans reduced-fat and reduced-sodium condensed cream of chicken soup
- ¾ cup water
- 1½ tsp. salt
- 1½ tsp. dried thyme, crushed
- ¼ tsp. black pepper
- 6 cups (12 oz.) dried wide noodles
- 1½ cups frozen peas

1 In a 5- to 6-quart slow cooker stir together carrots, onions, celery, and bay leaf. Place chicken on top of vegetables. In a large bowl stir together soup, the water, salt, thyme, and pepper. Pour over chicken in cooker. Cover and cook on low-heat setting for 8 to 9 hours or on high-heat setting for 4 to 4½ hours.

2 To serve, cook noodles according to package directions. Drain; return to pan. Cover and keep warm. Remove chicken from slow cooker; cool slightly. Discard bay leaf. Stir frozen peas into mixture in slow cooker. Remove and discard bones from chicken. Shred or chop chicken; stir into mixture in slow cooker.

3 In a large serving bowl combine chicken mixture and noodles.

Makes 9 servings

Per serving: 288 cal., 5 g total fat (2 g sat. fat), 69 mg chol., 680 mg sodium, 44 g carbo., 5 g fiber, 17 g pro.

Chicken and Orzo Casserole

Smoked paprika is made by smoking Spanish pimiento peppers over an oak fire. It's more expensive than ordinary paprika, but once you experience its deep flavor, you'll have no other.

Prep: 15 minutes   **Bake:** 20 minutes   **Stand:** 10 minutes   **Oven:** 350°F

4   tsp. cumin seeds

2   14.5-oz. cans stewed tomatoes, undrained

2   14-oz. cans chicken broth

2   cups (12 oz.) dried orzo pasta

½   cup oil-packed dried tomatoes, cut up

4   9-oz. pkg. southwest-flavored frozen cooked chicken breast strips, thawed

Smoked paprika (optional)

Seeded and chopped jalapeño chile peppers (optional) (see note, page 15)

1 Preheat oven to 350°F. In a large saucepan heat cumin seeds over medium heat for 3 to 4 minutes or until seeds are toasted and aromatic, shaking pan occasionally. Carefully stir in undrained tomatoes, broth, orzo, and tomatoes. Bring to boiling. Divide mixture between two 2-quart casseroles. Top with chicken strips. Cover casseroles.

2 Bake for 20 minutes or until orzo is tender. Let stand, covered, for 10 minutes before serving. If desired, top with paprika and jalapeño peppers.

Makes 8 to 12 servings

Per serving: 388 cal., 7 g total fat (2 g sat. fat), 60 mg chol., 1,227 mg sodium, 44 g carbo., 3 g fiber, 35 g pro.

Chicken Caesar Lasagna

Serve this delicious dish to introduce your family to healthful, fiber-rich whole wheat pasta.

Prep: 35 minutes   **Bake:** 50 minutes   **Stand:** 15 minutes   **Oven:** 325°F

9   dried whole wheat or regular lasagna noodles

2   10-oz. containers refrigerated light Alfredo pasta sauce

3   Tbsp. lemon juice

½   tsp. cracked black pepper

3   cups (about 15 oz.) chopped cooked chicken breast

1   10-oz. pkg. frozen chopped spinach, thawed and well drained

1   cup chopped bottled roasted red sweet peppers

Nonstick cooking spray

¾   cup (3 oz.) shredded Italian cheese blend

1 Preheat oven to 325°F. Cook noodles according to package directions. Drain; rinse with cold water; drain again. Meanwhile, in a bowl combine Alfredo sauce, lemon juice, and black pepper. Stir in chicken, spinach, and roasted red peppers.

2 Lightly coat a 3-quart rectangular baking dish with cooking spray. Arrange one-third of the noodles in bottom of dish. Top with one-third of the chicken mixture. Repeat layers twice. Cover with foil.

3 Bake for 45 to 55 minutes or until heated through. Uncover; sprinkle with cheese. Bake, uncovered, for 5 minutes more or until cheese is melted. Let stand for 15 minutes before serving.

Makes 9 servings

Per serving: 268 cal., 10 g total fat (6 g sat. fat), 68 mg chol., 557 mg sodium, 20 g carbo., 2 g fiber, 24 g pro.

Chicken Chow Mein Casserole

This family favorite travels well to potlucks. For a lower-sodium version, use reduced-sodium condensed chicken soup.

Prep: 25 minutes   **Bake:** 50 minutes   **Oven:** 350°F

- 4 cups chopped cooked chicken
- 2 cups chopped celery
- 1 cup shredded carrots
- 1 cup chopped green sweet pepper
- 2 4-oz. cans sliced mushrooms, drained
- ⅔ cup sliced or slivered almonds, toasted
- 2 Tbsp. diced pimiento, drained
- 2 10.75-oz. cans condensed cream of chicken soup
- 2 cups chow mein noodles

1 Preheat oven to 350°F. In a very large bowl stir together chicken, celery, carrots, sweet pepper, mushrooms, almonds, and pimiento. Add soup to chicken mixture; mix well.

2 Transfer chicken mixture to a 3-quart rectangular baking dish. Bake, covered, for 45 minutes. Uncover and top with chow mein noodles. Bake, uncovered, 5 to 10 minutes more or until heated through.

Makes 8 servings

Per serving: 366 cal., 19 g total fat (4 g sat. fat), 68 mg chol., 921 mg sodium, 21 g carbo., 4 g fiber, 27 g pro.

To tote: *Cover tightly. Transport in an insulated carrier.*

Florentine Chicken-Artichoke Bake

Frozen spinach holds a lot of liquid. To make sure that it is adequately drained, use the heel of your hand to firmly press spinach against the side of a colander until all liquid is released.

Prep: 30 minutes   **Bake:** 30 minutes   **Oven:** 350°F

7	cups (16 oz.) dried bow tie or rotini pasta
¼	cup butter
⅔	cup chopped onion
4	eggs
2½	cups milk
2	tsp. dried Italian seasoning, crushed
1	tsp. salt
½	tsp. black pepper
4	cups (about 1¼ lb.) chopped cooked chicken
4	cups (16 oz.) shredded Monterey Jack cheese
2	14-oz. cans artichoke hearts, drained and quartered
2	10-oz. pkg. frozen chopped spinach, thawed and well drained
1	cup oil-packed dried tomatoes, drained and chopped
½	cup grated Parmesan cheese
1	cup soft bread crumbs
1	tsp. paprika

1 Preheat oven to 350°F. Cook pasta according to package directions. Drain; set aside. Meanwhile, in a large skillet melt half of the butter over medium heat. Add onion; cook and stir about 5 minutes or until tender. Remove from heat; set aside.

2 In very large bowl whisk together eggs, milk, Italian seasoning, salt, and pepper. Stir in chicken, Monterey Jack cheese, artichoke hearts, spinach, tomatoes, and half the Parmesan cheese. Toss with cooked pasta and cooked onion mixture. Divide mixture between two 3-quart rectangular baking dishes. Cover with foil.

3 Bake for 20 minutes. Meanwhile, in a small saucepan melt remaining butter; remove from heat. Stir in the remaining Parmesan cheese, bread crumbs, and paprika. Sprinkle crumb mixture over pasta. Bake, uncovered, for 10 minutes more or until heated through.

Makes 12 servings

Per serving: 531 cal., 24 g total fat (13 g sat. fat), 163 mg chol., 897 mg sodium, 41 g carbo., 5 g fiber, 36 g pro.

Chicken Supreme Casserole

Mayonnaise is the ingredient that makes the sauce silky and the flavor unforgettable.

Prep: 25 minutes   **Bake:** 30 minutes   **Stand:** 10 minutes   **Oven:** 350°F

3¼ cups (8 oz.) dried rotini pasta

1 16-oz. pkg. frozen stir-fry vegetables (broccoli, carrots, onions, red peppers, celery, water chestnuts, and mushrooms)

2 10.75-oz. cans condensed cream of chicken soup

2 cups milk

¼ cup mayonnaise or salad dressing

¼ tsp. black pepper

2 cups (about 10 oz.) chopped cooked chicken

2 cups French bread cubes

2 Tbsp. butter or margarine, melted

¼ tsp. garlic powder

1 Tbsp. snipped fresh parsley

1 Preheat oven to 350°F. Cook rotini according to package directions, adding the stir-fry vegetables for the last 5 minutes of cooking; drain well.

2 Meanwhile, in a large bowl stir together soup, milk, mayonnaise, and pepper. Stir in cooked pasta mixture and chicken.

3 Transfer to a 3-quart rectangular baking dish. In a bowl toss together bread cubes, melted butter, and garlic powder; sprinkle over pasta mixture.

4 Bake, uncovered, for 30 to 35 minutes or until heated through and bread cubes are golden. Let stand for 10 minutes. Sprinkle with parsley.

Makes 6 to 8 servings

Per serving: 584 cal., 25 g total fat (8 g sat. fat), 71 mg chol., 1,123 mg sodium, 60 g carbo., 4 g fiber, 28 g pro.

Potluck Chicken Tetrazzini

This classic casserole was created in honor of the Italian opera singer Louisa Tetrazzini. One bite of its glorious richness will have taste buds singing.

Prep: 30 minutes   **Bake:** 15 minutes   **Stand:** 5 minutes   **Oven:** 350°F

8	oz. dried spaghetti or linguine, broken in half
12	oz. fresh asparagus, trimmed and cut into 1-inch pieces
2	Tbsp. butter
8	oz. small whole fresh mushrooms*
3	medium red and/or yellow sweet peppers, seeded and cut into 1-inch pieces
¼	cup all-purpose flour
⅛	tsp. black pepper
1	14-oz. can chicken broth
¾	cup milk
3	cups (about 15 oz.) chopped cooked chicken
½	cup (2 oz.) shredded Swiss cheese
1	Tbsp. finely shredded lemon peel
1½	cups sourdough bread cubes
1	Tbsp. olive oil
2	Tbsp. snipped fresh parsley

1 Preheat oven to 350°F. Cook spaghetti according to package directions, adding the asparagus for the last 1 minute of cooking. Drain; return to pan. Set aside.

2 Meanwhile, in large skillet melt butter over medium heat. Add mushrooms and sweet peppers; cook and stir in hot butter for 8 to 10 minutes or until mushrooms are tender. Stir in flour and black pepper. Add broth and milk. Cook and stir until thickened and bubbly.

3 Add mushroom mixture, chicken, cheese, and half the lemon peel to pasta; toss gently to coat. Transfer pasta mixture to a 3-quart rectangular baking dish.

4 In a bowl toss together bread cubes, oil, and the remaining lemon peel. Sprinkle bread cube mixture over pasta mixture.

5 Bake, uncovered, for 15 minutes or until heated through. Let stand for 5 minutes. Sprinkle with parsley.

Makes 10 servings

Per serving: 282 cal., 10 g total fat (4 g sat. fat), 48 mg chol., 258 mg sodium, 28 g carbo., 2 g fiber, 20 g pro.

---

*Note: *If mushrooms are large, cut them in half or in quarters so they are in pieces that are about 1 to 1½ inches.*

Lemon Chicken Pasta Toss

A bit more work but worth the effort, freshly squeezed lemon juice tastes much more alive than bottled versions. The juice adds zesty flavor to this quick-to-make dish.

Prep: 20 minutes   **Cook:** 20 minutes

- 2 cups (6 oz.) dried multigrain penne
- 12 oz. skinless, boneless chicken breasts, cut into 1-inch pieces
- 2 Tbsp. all-purpose flour
- 2 Tbsp. olive oil
- ⅓ cup finely chopped shallot
- 2 cloves garlic, minced
- ¾ cup chicken broth
- 3 Tbsp. lemon juice
- ¼ tsp. salt
- ¼ tsp. black pepper
- 1 halved yellow and/or red cherry tomatoes
- 3 Tbsp. capers, drained
- 3 Tbsp. snipped Italian (flat-leaf) parsley
- Freshly grated Parmesan cheese (optional)

1 Cook pasta according to package directions. Drain; return pasta to hot pan. Cover and keep warm.

2 Meanwhile, in a bowl toss together chicken and flour until chicken is lightly coated. In a large skillet heat half of the oil over medium-high heat. Add chicken; cook and stir for 6 to 8 minutes or until chicken is no longer pink. Remove chicken from skillet; set aside.

3 Reduce heat to medium. Add the remaining oil to skillet. Add shallot and garlic; cook and stir for 1 minute or until tender. Carefully stir in broth, lemon juice, salt, and pepper. Cook, uncovered, for 2 to 3 minutes or until reduced to about ⅔ cup. Stir in chicken, tomatoes, capers, and parsley; heat through.

4 Toss pasta with chicken mixture. If desired, serve with cheese.

Makes 4 servings

Per serving: 339 cal., 9 g total fat (1 g sat. fat), 50 mg chol., 589 mg sodium, 36 g carbo., 4 g fiber, 29 g pro.

Mediterranean Chicken and Pasta

Campanelle [kah-pah-NELL-eh] means "little bell" in Italian. The pasta has an open-vessel shape that holds the piquant artichoke marinade.

Start to Finish: 30 minutes

- 2   6-oz. jars marinated artichoke hearts
- 2   Tbsp. olive oil
- 1½   lb. skinless, boneless chicken breast halves, cut into ¾-inch cubes
- 6   cloves garlic, thinly sliced
- ½   cup chicken broth
- ½   cup dry white wine
- 2   7-oz. jars roasted red sweet peppers, drained and cut into strips
- ½   cup pitted kalamata olives
- 2   Tbsp. snipped fresh oregano
- 6   cups hot cooked campanelle or penne pasta
- ½   cup (2 oz.) crumbled feta cheese (optional)

1 Drain artichokes, reserving marinade. Set aside. In an extra-large skillet heat half of the oil over medium-high heat. Add half of the chicken and half of the garlic; cook and stir until chicken is brown. Using a slotted spoon remove chicken and garlic from skillet; set aside. Repeat with remaining oil, chicken, and garlic. Return all of the chicken and garlic to the skillet. Add the reserved artichoke marinade, broth, and wine.

2 Bring to boiling; reduce heat. Simmer, covered, for 10 minutes. Stir in artichokes, roasted red peppers, olives, and oregano. Heat through.

3 Serve the chicken mixture over hot cooked pasta. If desired, sprinkle with cheese.

Makes 8 servings

Per serving: 337 cal., 9 g total fat (1 g sat. fat), 49 mg chol., 323 mg sodium, 36 g carbo., 2 g fiber, 26 g pro.

Chicken-Broccoli Bake

Tried-and-true chicken and broccoli bake is a must for most potluck gatherings. Be sure to take enough!

Prep: 30 minutes   **Bake:** 55 minutes   **Oven:** 350°F

Nonstick cooking spray

10 oz. dried medium noodles

1½ lb. skinless, boneless chicken breast halves, cut into bite-size pieces

3 cups sliced fresh mushrooms

8 green onions, sliced

1 medium red sweet pepper, chopped

2 10.75-oz. cans condensed cream of broccoli soup

2 8-oz. cartons sour cream

⅓ cup chicken broth

2 tsp. dry mustard

¼ tsp. black pepper

1 16-oz. pkg. frozen chopped broccoli, thawed and drained

½ cup fine dry bread crumbs

2 Tbsp. butter or margarine, melted

1 Coat a 3-quart rectangular baking dish with cooking spray; set dish aside.

2 Cook noodles according to package directions; drain. Rinse with cold water; drain again.

3 Meanwhile, coat a large skillet with cooking spray. Heat over medium heat. Add chicken to skillet. Cook and stir about 3 minutes or until chicken is no longer pink. Transfer chicken from the skillet to a large bowl.

4 Preheat oven to 350°F. Add mushrooms, green onions, and sweet pepper to skillet. Cook and stir until vegetables are tender. (If necessary, add 1 tablespoon vegetable oil to skillet.)

5 Transfer vegetables to bowl with chicken. Stir in soup, sour cream, broth, mustard, and black pepper. Gently stir in cooked noodles and broccoli.

6 Spoon chicken mixture into prepared baking dish. Mix bread crumbs and melted butter; sprinkle over chicken mixture. Bake, covered, for 30 minutes. Uncover and bake about 25 minutes more or until heated through.

Makes 12 servings

Per serving: 336 cal., 15 g total fat (8 g sat. fat), 79 mg chol., 515 mg sodium, 29 g carbo., 3 g fiber, 21 g pro.

To tote: *Cover tightly. Transport in an insulated carrier.*

Chicken Fajita Pasta

Even the fussiest young eaters warm to foods flavored with Mexican spices. This kid-friendly recipe will be a popular request.

Start to Finish: 35 minutes

- 12 oz. dried pappardelle pasta or egg noodles
- 1 8-oz. carton sour cream
- ½ cup chipotle-flavor liquid meat marinade
- 2 Tbsp. lime juice
- 1 tsp. chili powder
- 1 tsp. ground cumin
- ½ tsp. crushed red pepper
- 2 Tbsp. olive oil
- 1 medium onion, halved and thinly sliced
- 1 medium red sweet pepper, cut into thin bite-size strips
- 1 fresh Anaheim chile pepper, seeded and cut into thin bite-size strips (see note, page 15)
- 3 large (1 to 1¼ lb. total) skinless, boneless chicken breast halves, cut into thin bite-size strips
- 1 Tbsp. snipped fresh cilantro (optional)
  Lime wedges (optional)

1 Cook pasta according to package directions. Drain and return pasta to pan. Cover and keep warm. Meanwhile, in a bowl combine sour cream, marinade, lime juice, chili powder, cumin, and crushed red pepper. Set aside.

2 In a large skillet heat half of the oil over medium heat. Add onion, sweet pepper, and Anaheim pepper; cook and stir for 4 to 5 minutes or until crisp-tender. Remove vegetables from skillet; set aside. Add remaining oil to skillet. Turn heat to medium-high. Add half of the chicken; cook and stir for 2 to 3 minutes or until chicken is no longer pink. Remove chicken from skillet; set aside. Repeat with remaining chicken (if necessary, add additional oil).

3 Add all of the chicken, the vegetables, and sour cream mixture to pasta. Toss to coat. Heat through over low heat. If desired, sprinkle with cilantro and serve with lime wedges.

Makes 6 to 8 servings

Per serving: 453 cal., 15 g total fat (6 g sat. fat), 60 mg chol., 589 mg sodium, 53 g carbo., 3 g fiber, 27 g pro.

Creamy Ranch Chicken

When your objective is making eaters absolutely ecstatic, remember these four words: Bring. On. The. Bacon.

Start to Finish: 30 minutes

- 6 cups (12 oz.) dried medium noodles
- 12 slices bacon, cut into narrow strips
- 8 medium (2 to 2½ lb. total) boneless chicken breast halves, cut into bite-size pieces
- ¼ cup all-purpose flour
- ¼ cup ranch dry salad dressing mix
- 2½ cups whole milk
- 2 Tbsp. finely shredded Parmesan cheese

1 Cook noodles according to package directions. Drain; return to pan. Cover and keep warm.

2 In an extra-large skillet cook bacon over medium heat until crisp. Drain bacon on paper towels; discard all but ¼ cup drippings.

3 In the same skillet cook and stir half of the chicken in reserved drippings until tender and no longer pink. Using a slotted spoon, remove chicken from skillet; set aside. Repeat with remaining chicken. Return all chicken to the skillet.

4 Sprinkle flour and salad dressing mix over the chicken; stir well. Stir in milk. Cook and stir until thickened and bubbly. Cook and stir for 1 minute more. Stir in bacon.

5 Serve chicken mixture with noodles; sprinkle with cheese.

Makes 8 servings

Per serving: 488 cal., 18 g total fat (7 g sat. fat), 137 mg chol., 574 mg sodium, 27 g carbo., 1 g fiber, 45 g pro.

Tex-Mex Chicken 'n' Rice

Rice appears twice in this crowd pleaser. The supportive cast of ingredients, including chile peppers, chili powder, and cumin, contributes to the Tex-Mex flavor.

Prep: 20 minutes   **Bake:** 25 minutes   **Stand:** 5 minutes   **Oven:** 425°F

- 1 cup chopped onion
- 2 Tbsp. olive oil
- 1 6.9-oz. pkg. chicken-flavored rice and vermicelli mix
- 1 cup uncooked long grain rice
- 2 14-oz. cans chicken broth
- 2½ cups water
- 4 cups chopped cooked chicken (see note, page 47)
- 4 medium tomatoes, chopped
- 1 4-oz. can diced green chile peppers, drained
- 2 tsp. dried basil, crushed
- 1 Tbsp. chili powder
- ¼ tsp. ground cumin
- ¼ tsp. black pepper
- 1 cup (4 oz.) shredded cheddar cheese

1 In a 3-quart saucepan cook onion in hot oil until tender. Stir in rice and vermicelli mix (including seasoning package) and uncooked long grain rice. Cook and stir for 2 minutes. Stir in broth and water. Bring to boiling; reduce heat. Simmer, covered, for 20 minutes (liquid will not be fully absorbed).

2 Transfer the rice mixture to a very large bowl. Stir in chicken, tomatoes, chile peppers, basil, chili powder, cumin, and black pepper. Transfer to a 3-quart casserole.

3 Bake, covered, in a 425°F oven for 25 minutes. Uncover and sprinkle with cheese. Let stand for 5 minutes before serving.

Makes 12 servings

Per serving: 287 cal., 10 g total fat (3 g sat. fat), 51 mg chol., 578 mg sodium, 28 g carbo., 2 g fiber, 21 g pro.

Make-ahead directions: *Prepare casserole; cover and chill up to 24 hours. Bake, covered, in 425°F oven about 40 minutes or until heated through. Uncover and sprinkle with cheese. Let stand for 5 minutes before serving.*

To tote: *Cover tightly after sprinkling with cheese. Transport in an insulated carrier.*

Sweet-and-Sour Baked Chicken

Baking makes classic sweet-and-sour chicken easier to make and more totable. For a family-size version, serve over hot cooked rice.

Prep: 25 minutes   **Bake:** 30 minutes   **Oven:** 350°F

- 8 medium skinless, boneless chicken breast halves
  Salt and black pepper
- 2 Tbsp. vegetable oil
- 1 20-oz. can pineapple chunks (juice pack)
- 1 cup jellied cranberry sauce
- ¼ cup cornstarch
- ¼ cup packed brown sugar
- ¼ cup rice vinegar or cider vinegar
- ¼ cup frozen orange juice concentrate, thawed
- ¼ cup dry sherry, chicken broth, or water
- ¼ cup soy sauce
- ½ tsp. ground ginger
- 2 medium green sweet peppers, cut into bite-size strips

1 Preheat oven to 350°F. Sprinkle chicken lightly with salt and pepper. Heat oil in a large skillet over medium-high heat. Add chicken and cook about 2 minutes on each side or until brown. (If necessary, brown chicken in batches.) Transfer chicken to a 3-quart rectangular baking dish. Drain pineapple well, reserving ⅔ cup juice. Spoon pineapple chunks evenly over chicken in dish; set aside.

2 For sauce, in a medium saucepan whisk together the reserved pineapple juice, the cranberry sauce, cornstarch, brown sugar, vinegar, orange juice concentrate, sherry, soy sauce, and ginger. Cook and stir over medium heat until thickened and bubbly. Pour over chicken and pineapple in dish.

3 Bake, covered, for 25 minutes. Uncover and add sweet pepper strips, stirring gently to coat with sauce. Bake, uncovered, about 5 minutes more or until chicken is no longer pink (170°F).

Makes 8 servings

Per serving: 368 cal., 6 g total fat (1 g sat. fat), 82 mg chol., 589 mg sodium, 41 g carbo., 2 g fiber, 35 g pro.

- -

To tote: *Cover tightly. Transport in an insulated carrier.*

Vegetable Chicken Lasagna

This cheesy yet healthful lasagna is full of rich nutrients from the spinach, tomatoes, and carrots, and best of all, it's lower in fat and calories compared to traditional lasagna.

Prep: 45 minutes **Bake:** 40 minutes **Stand:** 10 minutes **Oven:** 350°F

- 1 15-oz. carton ricotta cheese
- 1 10-oz. pkg. frozen chopped spinach, thawed and well drained
- 1 slightly beaten egg
- 2 tsp. dried Italian seasoning, crushed
- 1 lb. skinless, boneless chicken breast halves, cut into ½-inch pieces
- 3 cups sliced fresh mushrooms
- ½ cup chopped onion
- 1 Tbsp. olive oil
- 2 14.5-oz. cans diced tomatoes, undrained
- 1 8-oz. can tomato sauce
- 2 cups shredded carrots
- ½ tsp. black pepper
- 9 dried lasagna noodles
  Nonstick cooking spray
- 2 cups (8 oz.) shredded mozzarella cheese

1 For cheese filling, in a small bowl combine the ricotta cheese, spinach, egg, and half of the Italian seasoning. Cover and chill until ready to assemble lasagna.

2 Preheat oven to 350°F. For sauce, in a large skillet cook the chicken, mushrooms, onion, and the remaining Italian seasoning in hot oil for 4 to 5 minutes or until chicken is no longer pink. Stir in tomatoes, tomato sauce, carrots, and pepper. Bring to boiling; reduce heat. Simmer, uncovered, about 15 minutes or until slightly thickened, stirring occasionally.

3 Meanwhile, cook the lasagna noodles according to package directions. Drain noodles; rinse with cold water. Drain well.

4 Lightly coat a 3-quart rectangular baking dish with nonstick cooking spray. Place one-third of the lasagna noodles in prepared dish. Spread half of the cheese mixture over the noodles. Spread one-third of the sauce over the cheese mixture. Sprinkle with one-fourth of the mozzarella cheese. Repeat layers, ending with noodles. Spoon remaining sauce over the top. Sprinkle with the remaining mozzarella cheese.

5 Bake, covered, for 35 minutes. Uncover and bake for 5 to 10 minutes more or until cheese is bubbly. Let stand 10 minutes before serving.

Makes 8 to 10 servings

Per serving: 400 cal., 16 g total fat (8 g sat. fat), 102 mg chol., 552 mg sodium, 31 g carbo., 4 g fiber, 33 g pro.

To tote: *Do not let stand after baking. Cover tightly. Transport in an insulated carrier.*

Italian Chicken and Pasta

Thighs are the most succulent, flavorful part of the chicken. Unlike breasts, which become dry in a slow cooker, thighs remain moist and tender when cooked slowly for hours.

Prep: 20 minutes   **Cook:** 5 hours (low) or 2½ hours (high)

2 cups frozen Italian green beans or regular green beans

1 medium onion, cut into ¼-inch slices

1 cup fresh mushrooms, quartered

1 lb. skinless, boneless chicken thighs, cut into 1-inch pieces

1 15-oz. can tomato sauce

1 tsp. dried Italian seasoning, crushed

⅔ cup chopped roma tomatoes

2 cups hot cooked noodles

Finely shredded Parmesan cheese (optional)

1 In 3½- to 4-quart slow cooker combine beans, onion, and mushrooms. Place chicken on top of vegetables. In small bowl combine tomato sauce and Italian seasoning. Pour over chicken.

2 Cover and cook on low-heat setting for 5 to 6 hours or on high-heat setting for 2½ to 3 hours.

3 Stir in tomatoes. Serve chicken mixture over hot cooked noodles. If desired, sprinkle with cheese.

Makes 4 servings

Per serving: 318 cal., 7 g total fat (2 g sat. fat), 117 mg chol., 614 mg sodium, 33 g carbo., 4 g fiber, 30 g pro.

Red Chicken Enchiladas

Shredded chicken, which is simmered in onion, cilantro, and spices, makes up the filling for these party-worthy enchiladas.

Prep: 1 hour **Bake:** 20 minutes **Stand:** 5 minutes **Oven:** 350°F

- 1½ lb. skinless, boneless chicken breast halves
- 1 cup chopped onion
- ½ cup loosely packed fresh cilantro
- 1 tsp. crushed red pepper
- 2 fresh jalapeño chile peppers, seeded and chopped (see note, page 15)
- 2 tsp. chili powder
- 1 clove garlic, minced
- 1 Tbsp. vegetable oil
- 1 19-oz. can enchilada sauce
- 10 6-inch corn tortillas
- 1 cup (4 oz.) shredded Monterey Jack or cheddar cheese
- ½ cup sliced pitted ripe olives
- Sour cream (optional)
- 3 green onions, thinly sliced (optional)

1 In a large saucepan combine chicken, half of the onion, the cilantro, half of the crushed red pepper, half of the chopped jalapeño peppers, the chili powder, and garlic. Add enough water to cover chicken. Bring to boiling; reduce heat. Simmer, covered, for 15 to 20 minutes or until chicken is no longer pink (170°F). Drain well. When cool enough to handle, use a fork to shred chicken into bite-size pieces.

2 In a large skillet heat the oil over medium-high heat. Add remaining onion, remaining crushed red pepper, and remaining chopped jalapeño peppers. Reduce heat; cook and stir over low heat about 2 minutes or until onion is tender. Add shredded chicken and ½ cup of the enchilada sauce to skillet. Bring to boiling; reduce heat. Simmer, covered, for 10 minutes, stirring occasionally.

3 Preheat oven to 350°F. Spoon about ⅓ cup of the chicken mixture onto each tortilla near one edge; roll up. Place filled tortillas, seam sides down, in a lightly greased 2-quart rectangular baking dish. Pour remaining enchilada sauce over all.

4 Bake, covered, for 20 to 25 minutes or until heated through. Uncover and sprinkle with cheese. Let stand for 5 minutes before serving. Sprinkle with olives and, if desired, top with sour cream and green onions.

Makes 10 enchiladas

Per enchilada: 234 cal., 8 g total fat (3 g sat. fat), 49 mg chol., 519 mg sodium, 19 g carbo., 3 g fiber, 21 g pro.

To tote: *Cover tightly after sprinkling with cheese. Transport in an insulated carrier. Transport olives, and, if desired, green onions and sour cream in an insulated cooler with ice packs.*

Mexican-Style Chicken

Layered with tortilla strips, a tomatoey sauce, chicken, and cheddar cheese, this casserole will melt the hearts of Mexican food fans.

Prep: 20 minutes   **Bake:** 45 minutes   **Stand:** 10 minutes   **Oven:** 350°F

- 2 10¾-oz. cans reduced-sodium condensed cream of chicken soup
- 1 10-oz. can diced tomatoes with green chiles, undrained
- ¾ cup chopped green sweet pepper
- ½ cup chopped onion
- 1½ tsp. chili powder
- ¼ tsp. black pepper
- 12 6- or 7-inch corn tortillas, cut into thin bite-size strips
- 3 cups cubed cooked chicken*
- 1 8-oz. pkg. (2 cups) shredded cheddar cheese

   Tomato slices (optional)

   Sliced green onions (optional)

1 Preheat oven to 350°F. Combine soup, tomatoes with chiles, sweet pepper, onion, chili powder, and black pepper; set aside.

2 To assemble, sprinkle about one-third of the tortilla strips over the bottom of an ungreased 3-quart rectangular baking dish. Layer half of the chicken over tortilla strips; spoon half of soup mixture on top. Sprinkle half of the cheese and another one-third of the tortilla strips over the soup mixture. Layer with remaining chicken, soup mixture, and tortilla strips.

3 Bake, uncovered, about 45 minutes or until bubbly around edges and center is hot. Remove from oven; sprinkle with remaining cheese. Let stand 10 minutes before serving. If desired, top with sliced tomatoes and green onions.

Makes 8 servings

Per serving: 380 cal., 16 g total fat (7 g sat. fat), 83 mg chol., 702 mg sodium, 33 g carbo., 2 g fiber, 27 g pro.

To tote: *Cover tightly after sprinkling with cheese. Transport in an insulated carrier. If desired, transport tomatoes and green onions in an insulated cooler with ice packs.*

---

*Note: *About 1 pound boneless chicken breasts will yield 3 cups cubed cooked chicken.*

Tortellini Vegetable Bake

Use refrigerated—not dried—tortellini for this chicken-pasta bake. Cream cheese and a little lemon juice add a slight tang to the creamy sauce.

Prep: 30 minutes   **Bake:** 30 minutes   **Oven:** 350°F

2	9-oz. pkgs. refrigerated tortellini
1½	cups sugar snap peas, trimmed and halved crosswise
½	cup thinly sliced carrot
1	Tbsp. butter or margarine
1	lb. skinless, boneless chicken breast halves, cut into bite-size pieces
1	cup sliced fresh mushrooms
⅓	cup chicken broth
2	tsp. all-purpose flour
1½	tsp. dried oregano, crushed
½	tsp. garlic salt
½	tsp. black pepper
1	cup milk
1	8-oz. pkg. cream cheese, cubed and softened
1	Tbsp. lemon juice
1	cup quartered cherry tomatoes
½	cup coarsely chopped red or green sweet pepper
2	Tbsp. grated Parmesan cheese

1 Preheat oven to 350°F. Cook tortellini according to package directions, adding the sugar snap peas and the carrot during the last 1 minute of cooking; drain well.

2 Meanwhile, melt butter in an extra-large skillet; add chicken and mushrooms. Cook and stir about 5 minutes or until chicken is no longer pink. Remove from skillet.

3 In a screw-top jar combine chicken broth, flour, oregano, garlic salt, and pepper. Cover and shake until smooth. Add to skillet along with milk. Cook and stir until thickened and bubbly; add cream cheese. Cook and stir until cream cheese is smooth. Remove from heat; stir in lemon juice. Stir in pasta mixture, chicken mixture, tomatoes, and sweet pepper. Transfer to an ungreased 3-quart rectangular baking dish.

4 Bake, covered, about 30 minutes or until heated through. Sprinkle with Parmesan cheese.

Makes 8 servings

Per serving: 420 cal., 18 g total fat (10 g sat. fat), 101 mg chol., 501 mg sodium, 37 g carbo., 1 g fiber, 28 g pro.

To tote: *Transport in an insulated carrier.*

Taco Pasta

Hungry for Mexican food? This combination of pasta, salsa, ground chicken, and cheese will satisfy your craving.

Prep: 20 minutes   **Bake:** 45 minutes   **Oven:** 350°F

- 8   oz. dried penne
- 2   lb. uncooked ground chicken
- 1   cup chopped onion
- 1½   cups water
- 1   1.25-oz. envelope taco seasoning mix
- 2   11-oz. cans whole kernel corn with sweet peppers, drained
- 2   cups sliced pitted ripe olives
- 2   cups (8 oz.) shredded cheddar cheese
- 1   cup salsa
- 2   4-oz. cans diced green chile peppers, drained
- 8   cups shredded lettuce
- 2   medium tomatoes, cut into thin wedges
- Tortilla chips (optional)
- Sour cream (optional)

1 Preheat oven to 350°F. Cook pasta according to directions; drain and set aside.

2 Meanwhile, in an extra-large skillet cook ground chicken and onion, half at a time, until meat is brown; drain fat. Return all of the chicken mixture to skillet. Stir in water and taco seasoning mix. Bring to boiling; reduce heat. Simmer, uncovered, for 2 minutes, stirring occasionally. Stir in cooked pasta, corn, olives, half of the shredded cheese, salsa, and chile peppers.

3 Transfer mixture to a lightly greased 3-quart rectangular casserole. Bake, covered, about 45 minutes or until heated through. Remove from oven; sprinkle with remaining cheese.

4 Serve with lettuce, tomato wedges, and, if desired, tortilla chips and sour cream.

Makes 12 servings

Per serving: 351 cal., 17 g total fat (4 g sat. fat), 20 mg chol., 934 mg sodium, 30 g carbo., 4 g fiber, 24 g pro.

- -

To tote: *Cover tightly. Transport in an insulated carrier. Transport lettuce, tomatoes, and, if desired, sour cream in an insulated cooler with ice packs. If desired, transport chips in an airtight bag or container.*

Chicken and Herbed Dressing Casserole

This tasty dressing is made in a slow cooker, making it an easy dish to transport to a holiday party.

Prep: 25 minutes   **Cook:** 3½ hours (low)

- 4½ cups sliced fresh mushrooms
- 1 cup sliced celery
- 1 cup chopped onion
- ⅓ cup butter or margarine
- ⅓ cup snipped fresh basil
- ½ tsp. black pepper
- 12 cups dry bread cubes
- 3 cups coarsely chopped cooked chicken or turkey
- 1 14-oz. can chicken broth
- ¾ cup chopped pecans, toasted

1 In a large skillet cook mushrooms, celery, and onion in hot butter over medium heat for 5 minutes. Remove from heat; stir in basil and pepper. Combine mushroom mixture, dry bread cubes, and cooked chicken. Add chicken broth to moisten, tossing gently. Spoon chicken mixture into a 5- to 6-quart slow cooker. Cover and cook on low-heat setting for 3½ to 4 hours. Just before serving, gently stir in nuts.

Makes 10 servings

Per serving: 356 cal., 18 g total fat (6 g sat. fat), 58 mg chol., 509 mg sodium, 29 g carbo., 3 g fiber, 20 g pro.

To tote: *Transport slow cooker and nuts in an insulated carrier. (Or, if desired, transfer hot mixture to a serving dish. Cover tightly. Transport in an insulated carrier.)*

Test Kitchen Tip: *To make 12 cups of dry cubes, cut 20 to 22 slices of bread into ½-inch cubes. Spread cubes in a single layer in a large, shallow baking pan. Bake, uncovered, in a 300°F oven for 10 to 15 minutes or until dry, stirring twice; cool. (Bread will continue to dry and crisp as it cools.)*

Baked Chicken Marsala

To tote to a party, leave cheeses and green onions off during the baking time. When you reach your destination, sprinkle the chicken with both and warm in the oven until cheese melts.

Prep: 30 minutes   **Bake:** 20 minutes   **Oven:** 375°F

- 8 medium skinless, boneless chicken breast halves
- ⅓ cup all-purpose flour
- 6 Tbsp. butter or margarine
- 2 cups sliced fresh mushrooms
- 1 cup dry Marsala
- ⅔ cup chicken broth
- ⅛ tsp. salt
- ⅛ tsp. black pepper
- 1 cup (4 oz.) shredded mozzarella or fontina cheese
- ⅔ cup grated Parmesan cheese
- ½ cup thinly sliced green onions

1 Cut each breast half in half lengthwise. Place each chicken piece between 2 pieces of plastic wrap. Using the flat side of a meat mallet, pound each piece to ⅛ inch thick. Remove plastic wrap. Coat chicken lightly with flour.

2 In an extra-large skillet melt 1 tablespoon of the butter over medium heat. Add four of the chicken pieces. Cook for 2 minutes on each side. Transfer to a 3-quart rectangular baking dish. Repeat with remaining butter and chicken pieces.

3 Preheat oven to 375°F. Melt the remaining 2 tablespoons butter in the skillet; add mushrooms. Cook and stir until tender; stir in Marsala, broth, salt, and pepper. Bring to boiling; boil gently about 5 minutes or until mixture is reduced to 1 cup (including the mushrooms). Pour over the chicken.

4 Combine mozzarella cheese, Parmesan cheese, and green onions; sprinkle over the chicken. Bake, uncovered, about 20 minutes or until chicken is no longer pink (170°F).

Makes 8 servings

Per serving: 364 cal., 17 g total fat (9 g sat. fat), 121 mg chol., 496 mg sodium, 6 g carbo., 0 g fiber, 42 g pro.

To tote: *Cover tightly. Transport in an insulated carrier.*

Spinach-Stuffed Chicken Rolls

Serve this chicken warm or cold. Either way it's an impressive dish to take to your next potluck or party.

Prep: 40 minutes   **Bake:** 20 minutes   **Oven:** 350°F

- ⅔ cup chopped onion
- ⅔ cup chopped fresh mushrooms
- 2 cloves garlic, minced
- 2 Tbsp. butter or margarine
- 1 10-oz. pkg. frozen chopped spinach, thawed and well drained
- ¾ tsp. dried oregano, crushed
- ½ tsp. salt
- ¼ tsp. black pepper
- 8 medium skinless, boneless chicken breast halves
- ⅔ cup fine dry bread crumbs
- ¼ cup grated Parmesan cheese
- ½ tsp. paprika
- 2 slightly beaten eggs
- 1 Tbsp. water
- 3 Tbsp. butter or margarine, melted

1 For filling, in a large skillet cook onion, mushrooms, and garlic in the 2 tablespoons hot butter until tender. Stir in spinach, oregano, salt, and pepper; set filling aside.

2 Place each chicken breast half between two pieces of plastic wrap. Using the flat side of a meat mallet, pound each chicken breast lightly into a rectangle about ⅛ inch thick. Remove plastic wrap.

3 Divide the filling evenly among the chicken breast halves. Fold in sides; roll up. If necessary, secure with wooden toothpicks.

4 Preheat oven to 350°F. In a shallow dish combine bread crumbs, Parmesan cheese, and paprika. In another shallow dish combine beaten egg and water. Dip chicken rolls in the egg mixture; coat with bread crumb mixture. Place rolls, seam sides down, in a lightly greased 3-quart rectangular baking dish. Drizzle with the melted butter.

5 Bake, uncovered, for 20 to 25 minutes or until chicken is no longer pink (170°F).

Makes 8 servings

Per serving: 287 cal., 11 g total fat (6 g sat. fat), 105 mg chol., 569 mg sodium, 811 g carbo., 2 g fiber, 37 g pro.

To tote: *Cover tightly. Transport in an insulated carrier.*

Chiles Rellenos Chicken

In this recipe, classic cheese-stuffed chile pepper is rolled up in chicken. Serve along with Spanish-style rice and refried beans for a Mexican-inspired meal.

Prep: 25 minutes   **Bake:** 40 minutes   **Oven:** 375°F

8	medium skinless, boneless chicken breast halves
1	cup (4 oz.) shredded taco cheese or cheddar cheese
¼	cup finely chopped onion
¼	cup snipped fresh cilantro (optional)
2	tsp. chili powder
8	canned whole green chile peppers, drained
2	beaten eggs
2	Tbsp. milk
½	cup fine dry bread crumbs
1	tsp. salt

1 Place each chicken breast half between two pieces of plastic wrap. Using the flat side of a meat mallet, pound each chicken breast lightly to about ¼ inch thick. Remove plastic wrap. Set chicken aside.

2 In a small bowl combine the cheese, onion, cilantro (if desired), and half of the chili powder. Stuff some of the cheese mixture into each whole chile pepper.

3 Preheat oven to 375°F. Place a stuffed pepper on top of each flattened chicken breast. Roll up chicken around pepper, folding in sides. If necessary, secure with wooden toothpicks.

4 In a shallow dish combine the eggs and milk. In another shallow dish stir together the bread crumbs, the remaining chili powder, and salt. Dip chicken rolls in egg mixture; coat with bread crumb mixture.

5 Place chicken rolls in an ungreased 3-quart rectangular baking dish. Bake, uncovered, about 40 minutes or until chicken is no longer pink (170°F).

Makes 8 servings

Per serving: 266 cal., 4 g total fat (4 g sat. fat), 149 mg chol., 720 mg sodium, 6 g carbo., 1 g fiber, 36 g pro.

- -

Make-ahead directions: *Prepare as directed. Cover and chill for up to 2 hours. Bake as directed.*

- -

To tote: *Cover tightly. Transport in an insulated carrier.*

Cajun Chicken Lasagna

Tired of plain lasagna? This version, spiced up with Cajun seasoning and andouille sausage, will surely become a perennial favorite.

Prep: 45 minutes   **Bake:** 1 hour   **Stand:** 15 minutes   **Oven:** 350°F

16	dried lasagna noodles
1	lb. cooked andouille sausage or smoked pork sausage, quartered lengthwise and sliced
1	lb. skinless, boneless chicken breast halves, cut into ¾-inch pieces
2	to 3 tsp. Cajun seasoning
1	tsp. dried sage, crushed
½	cup chopped onion
½	cup chopped celery
¼	cup chopped green sweet pepper
6	cloves garlic, minced
2	10-oz. containers refrigerated Alfredo sauce
½	cup grated Parmesan cheese
	Nonstick cooking spray
1½	cups (6 oz.) shredded mozzarella cheese

1 Cook lasagna noodles according to package directions. Drain noodles; rinse with cold water. Drain well.

2 Meanwhile, in a bowl combine sausage, chicken, Cajun seasoning, and sage. In a large skillet cook and stir chicken mixture about 8 minutes or until chicken is no longer pink. Using a slotted spoon, remove chicken mixture from skillet, reserving drippings in skillet. Set chicken mixture aside. In the same skillet cook onion, celery, sweet pepper, and garlic in drippings until vegetables are tender. Return chicken mixture to skillet; stir in half of the Alfredo sauce and the Parmesan cheese.

3 Preheat oven to 350°F. Lightly coat a 3-quart rectangular baking dish with cooking spray. Place one-fourth of the noodles in the bottom of the dish, cutting as necessary to fit. Spread with one-third of the chicken-vegetable mixture. Sprinkle with one-third of the mozzarella cheese. Repeat layers twice; top with remaining noodles. Carefully spread remaining Alfredo sauce over the top.

4 Bake, covered, about 1 hour or until heated through. Let stand for 15 to 20 minutes before serving.

Makes 12 servings

Per serving: 507 cal., 31 g total fat (7 g sat. fat), 83 mg chol., 938 mg sodium, 27 g carbo., 1 g fiber, 29 g pro.

To tote: *Do not let stand after baking. Cover tightly. Transport in an insulated carrier.*

Cheesy Corn and Chicken Turnovers

Impress family and friends with this easy version of Latin empanadas. The light and flaky crust surrounds the hearty fillings in the little pies.

Prep: 35 minutes   **Bake:** 15 minutes   **Oven:** 400°F

- 4 cups (about 1¼ lb.) chopped cooked chicken
- 2 11-oz. cans whole kernel corn with sweet peppers, drained
- 2 10.75-oz. cans condensed cream of chicken with herbs soup or cream of mushroom soup
- 2 cups (8 oz.) shredded cheddar cheese
- 2 15-ounce pkg. (2 crusts each) rolled refrigerated unbaked piecrust
  Water

1 Preheat oven to 400°F. Grease two large baking sheets; set aside. In a bowl combine chicken, corn, soup, and cheese. Unroll piecrusts according to package directions. On a lightly floured surface, roll each piecrust into a 13-inch circle. Cut each piecrust into quarters. Spoon about ½ cup of the chicken mixture along one straight side of each quarter about ¾ inch from edge.

2 Brush edges of pastry quarters with water. Fold the other straight side of each quarter over the filling. Seal edges with the tines of a fork and prick the top of each turnover several times. Place turnovers on prepared baking sheets. Bake about 15 minutes or until turnovers are golden. Serve hot.

Makes 8 servings

Per serving: 862 cal., 47 g total fat (21 g sat. fat), 118 mg chol., 1,625 mg sodium, 73 g carbo., 3 g fiber, 33 g pro.

Chicken and Wild Rice Casserole

For potluck dinners, let guests serve themselves out of the baking dish. For a more special presentation at home, spoon hot portions of the casserole into steamed fresh sweet pepper halves.

Prep: 35 minutes **Bake:** 35 minutes **Oven:** 350°F

- 2 6-oz. pkgs. long grain and wild rice mix
- 6 cups chopped cooked chicken
- 2 14½-oz. cans French-cut green beans, drained
- 2 10¾-oz. cans condensed cream of celery soup
- 2 8-oz. cans sliced water chestnuts, drained
- 1 cup mayonnaise or salad dressing
- 1 cup chopped onion
- ⅓ cup sliced almonds
- 1 4-oz. jar sliced pimientos, drained
- 2 tsp. lemon juice
- 2 cups (8 oz.) shredded cheddar cheese

1 Preheat oven to 350°F. Prepare rice according to package directions. Meanwhile, in a very large bowl combine chicken, green beans, celery soup, water chestnuts, mayonnaise, onion, almonds, pimientos, and lemon juice. Stir in cooked rice. Divide mixture between two 3-quart rectangular baking dishes.

2 Bake, covered, for 30 minutes. Uncover and sprinkle with cheese. Bake about 5 minutes more or until heated through and cheese is melted.

Makes 16 to 20 servings

Per serving: 406 cal., 23 g total fat (6 g sat. fat), 75 mg chol., 1,048 mg sodium, 25 g carbo., 2 g fiber, 24 g pro.

Make-ahead directions: *Prepare as directed. Cover and chill for up to 24 hours. Bake casserole, covered, in a 350°F oven for 45 minutes. Uncover and sprinkle with cheese. Bake about 5 minutes more or until heated through and cheese is melted.*

To tote: *Cover tightly. Transport in an insulated carrier.*

Turkey-Spinach Casserole

For a potluck or party, use a large baking dish. For a smaller party or dinner at home, au gratin dishes are more elegant.

Prep: 30 minutes   **Bake:** 25 minutes   **Oven:** 350°F

2   10-oz. pkgs. frozen chopped spinach or chopped broccoli

2   10.75-oz. cans reduced-fat and reduced-sodium condensed cream of celery, chicken, mushroom, or broccoli soup

2   cups water

¼   cup butter or margarine

6   cups herb-seasoned stuffing mix

4   cups chopped cooked turkey or chicken

⅔   cup milk

2   Tbsp. grated Parmesan cheese

1 Preheat oven to 350°F. In a Dutch oven or large saucepan combine spinach, half of the soup, the water, and butter. Bring to boiling. (If using spinach, separate it with a fork.) Cover and simmer for 5 minutes.

2 Add the stuffing mix to saucepan; stir to moisten. Spread mixture in an ungreased 3-quart rectangular baking dish or eight 10-ounce au gratin dishes; top with turkey. Stir milk into remaining soup; pour over turkey. Sprinkle with Parmesan cheese. Bake, uncovered, about 25 minutes or until heated through.

Makes 8 servings

Per serving: 375 cal., 12 g total fat (5 g sat. fat), 65 mg chol., 1065 mg sodium, 44 g carbo., 5 g fiber, 23 g pro.

To tote: *Cover tightly. Transport in an insulated carrier.*

One-Dish Turkey and Bis

*The ideal recipe for the day after Thanksgiving,
this quick-fix casserole turns leftover turkey into
a delicious treat.*

Prep: 30 minutes   **Bake:** 20 minutes   **Oven:** 425°F

1⅓ cups chicken broth

¾ cup finely chopped onion

⅔ cup finely chopped celery

2 cups frozen peas and carrots

1⅓ cups milk

¼ cup all-purpose flour

2⅔ cups (about 13 oz.) cubed cooked turkey breast

¾ tsp. dried sage, crushed

⅛ tsp. black pepper

1⅔ cups packaged biscuit mix

⅔ cup milk

1 Tbsp. dried parsley flakes, crushed

1 Preheat oven to 425°F. In a saucepan combine broth, onion, and celery. Bring to boiling; reduce heat. Cover and simmer for 5 minutes. Add peas and carrots; return to boiling.

2 In a bowl stir the 1⅓ cups milk into flour until well mixed; stir into vegetable mixture in saucepan. Cook and stir until thickened and bubbly. Stir in turkey, sage, and pepper. Transfer to a 3-quart casserole.

3 In a bowl combine biscuit mix, the ⅔ cup milk, and parsley flakes. Stir with a fork just until moistened. Spoon into 12 mounds on top of the hot turkey mixture in casserole.

4 Bake, uncovered, for 20 to 25 minutes or until biscuits are golden.

Makes 6 servings

Per serving: 356 cal., 8 g total fat (3 g sat. fat), 67 mg chol., 844 mg sodium, 41 g carbo., 3 g fiber, 30 g pro.

Nacho Turkey Casserole

If you enjoy nachos with all the fixings, you'll love this no-fuss casserole. Prep in 15 minutes, bake in 30 minutes—ole!!

Prep: 15 minutes   **Bake:** 30 minutes   **Oven:** 350°F

- 5 cups slightly crushed tortilla chips
- 4 cups cubed cooked turkey or chicken
- 2 16-oz. jars salsa
- 1 10-oz. pkg. frozen whole kernel corn
- ½ cup dairy sour cream
- 2 Tbsp. all-purpose flour
- 1 cup (4 oz.) shredded Monterey Jack cheese with jalapeño peppers or mozzarella cheese

  Fresh jalapeño chile pepper, thinly sliced (optional) (see note, page 15)

1 Preheat oven to 350°F. Lightly grease a 3-quart rectangular baking dish. Place 3 cups of the tortilla chips in bottom of dish. In a large bowl combine turkey, salsa, corn, sour cream, and flour; spoon over tortilla chips.

2 Bake, uncovered, for 25 minutes. Sprinkle with the remaining 2 cups tortilla chips and the cheese. Bake, uncovered, for 5 to 10 minutes more or until heated through. If desired, garnish with jalapeño slices.

Makes 8 servings

Per serving: 444 cal., 17 g total fat (7 g sat. fat), 74 mg chol., 1,127 mg sodium, 46 g carbo., 4 g fiber, 29 g pro.

To tote: *Cover tightly. Transport in an insulated carrier.*

Cheesy Turkey-Spinach Pie

Packages of fresh herbs usually contain more leaves than you can use in one recipe. To store extra herbs, place herb stems in a glass of water, cover loosely with a plastic bag, and refrigerate.

Prep: 30 minutes   **Bake:** 45 minutes   **Stand:** 10 minutes   **Oven:** 350°F

Nonstick cooking spray

3½ cups (8 oz.) dried fine noodles

6 eggs, beaten

2 8-oz. pkg. cream cheese or marscapone cheese, softened

⅔ cup sour cream

⅔ cup mayonnaise or salad dressing

½ cup snipped fresh basil

1 tsp. garlic salt

½ tsp. crushed red pepper

4 cups (about 1¼ lb.) chopped cooked turkey

2 10-oz. pkg. frozen chopped spinach, thawed and well drained

2 cups (8 oz.) shredded Monterey Jack cheese

⅔ cup chopped bottled roasted red sweet peppers

1 Preheat oven to 350°F. Coat two 9-inch deep-dish pie plates or two 2-quart square baking dishes with cooking spray; place plates or dishes on baking sheets. Set aside. Cook noodles according to package directions; drain well.

2 Meanwhile, in a large bowl whisk together eggs, cream cheese, sour cream, mayonnaise, basil, garlic salt, and crushed red pepper until well combined. Stir in cooked noodles, turkey, spinach, Monterey Jack cheese, and roasted red peppers. Divide mixture between prepared plates or dishes (pie plates will be very full).

3 Bake, uncovered, for 45 to 50 minutes or until edges are slightly puffed and golden. Let stand for 10 minutes before serving.

Makes 12 to 16 servings

Per serving: 520 cal., 37 g total fat (17 g sat. fat), 225 mg chol., 481 mg sodium, 18 g carbo., 3 g fiber, 29 g pro.

Popover Pizza Casserole

Be sure that the ground turkey you purchase for this recipe is 100 percent breast meat. Products labeled ground turkey contain a large percentage of unskinned dark meat and may contain excess fat.

Prep: 35 minutes   **Bake:** 30 minutes   **Oven:** 400°F

- 1¼ lb. ground uncooked turkey breast or extra-lean ground beef
- 2 cups sliced fresh mushrooms
- 1½ cups chopped yellow summer squash
- 1 cup chopped onion
- 1 cup chopped green sweet pepper
- 1 14- to 15-oz. jar or can pizza sauce
- 1 tsp. dried Italian seasoning, crushed
- ½ tsp. fennel seeds, crushed
- 1 cup milk
- 2 eggs
- 1 Tbsp. vegetable oil
- 1 cup all-purpose flour
- 1 cup (4 oz.) mozzarella cheese
- 2 Tbsp. grated Parmesan cheese

1 Preheat oven to 400°F. In an oven-going large skillet cook turkey, mushrooms, squash, onion, and sweet pepper over medium heat until turkey is brown and vegetables are tender, stirring to break up turkey. Drain off fat. Stir pizza sauce, Italian seasoning, and fennel seeds into turkey mixture. Bring to boiling; reduce heat. Simmer, uncovered, for 5 minutes, stirring occasionally. Spread to an even layer in skillet.

2 Meanwhile, for topping, in a bowl combine milk, eggs, and oil. Beat with an electric mixer on medium speed or whisk for 1 minute. Add flour; beat or whisk about 1 minute more or until smooth.

3 Sprinkle mozzarella cheese over meat mixture in skillet. Pour topping evenly over mixture in skillet, covering completely. Sprinkle with Parmesan cheese.

4 Bake, uncovered, for 30 to 35 minutes or until topping is puffed and golden. (Casserole may look a bit gooey on top of the turkey mixture from the melted cheese.) Serve immediately.

Makes 6 servings

Per serving: 360 cal., 11 g total fat (4 g sat. fat), 131 mg chol., 612 mg sodium, 31 g carbo., 3 g fiber, 35 g pro.

Turkey Manicotti with Chive Cream Sauce

A simple cream cheese sauce makes these pasta shells filled with turkey and broccoli elegant enough for a special gathering.

Prep: 30 minutes   **Bake:** 30 minutes   **Oven:** 350°F

- 12   dried manicotti shells
- 1   8-oz. tub cream cheese with chive and onion
- ⅔   cup milk
- ¼   cup grated Romano or Parmesan cheese
- 2   cups chopped cooked turkey or chicken
- 1   10-oz. pkg. frozen chopped broccoli, thawed and drained
- 1   4-oz. jar diced pimiento, drained
- ¼   tsp. black pepper

1 Preheat oven to 350°F. Cook manicotti according to package directions; drain. Rinse with cold water; drain again. Cool manicotti in a single layer on a piece of greased foil.

2 Meanwhile, for sauce, in a heavy small saucepan heat cream cheese over medium-low heat until melted, stirring constantly. Slowly stir in milk until smooth. Stir in Romano cheese.

3 For filling, combine ¾ cup of the sauce, the turkey, broccoli, pimiento, and pepper. Using a small spoon, carefully fill each manicotti shell with ¼ to ⅓ cup filling.

4 Arrange filled shells in a 3-quart rectangular baking dish. Pour remaining sauce over shells. Bake, covered, for 30 to 35 minutes or until heated through.

Makes 6 servings

Per serving: 381 cal., 17 g total fat (10 g sat. fat), 78 mg chol., 256 mg sodium, 32 g carbo., 3 g fiber, 22 g pro.

To tote: *Transport in an insulated carrier.*

Smoked Turkey Jambalaya

Creole flavors—bright and robust—burst from this savory concoction of mixed meats, summer vegetables, and tender white rice.

Prep: 30 minutes   **Bake:** 55 minutes   **Oven:** 350°F

- 4   cups water
- 2   cups long grain rice
- 2   16-oz. pkg. frozen peppers and onion stir-fry vegetables
- 2   14.5-oz. cans diced tomatoes with green pepper, celery, and onions, undrained
- 2   10-oz. cans diced tomatoes and green chiles, undrained
- 1   lb. turkey kielbasa or other smoked turkey sausage, cut into ¼-inch rounds
- 1   cup sliced green onions
- 1   tsp. Cajun seasoning
- 2   cloves garlic, minced
   Bottled hot pepper sauce

1 Preheat oven to 350°F. In a saucepan combine water and uncooked rice. Bring to boiling; reduce heat. Cover and simmer for 15 to 18 minutes or until rice is tender and water is absorbed.

2 In a large bowl combine rice, frozen vegetables, undrained tomatoes with green pepper, and undrained tomatoes with green chiles. Stir in kielbasa, green onions, Cajun seasoning, and garlic. Mix well. Divide between two 2-quart square baking dishes.

3 Bake, uncovered, about 55 minutes or until heated through, stirring once. Pass hot pepper sauce.

Makes 12 servings

Per serving: 219 cal., 3 g total fat (0 g sat. fat), 0 mg chol., 842 mg sodium, 35 g carbo., 3 g fiber, 12 g pro.

Picadillo Sandwiches, page 169

Chapter 3

Family-Approved
Meat
Dishes

Hamburger Pie

This hearty casserole has been a family favorite for decades.

Prep: 30 minutes   **Bake:** 30 minutes   **Oven:** 350°F

2½ lb. lean ground beef

1 cup chopped onion

½ tsp. salt

Several dashes black pepper

5 cups frozen cut green beans, thawed

2 10.75-oz. cans condensed tomato soup

2 24-oz. pkg. refrigerated mashed potatoes

1 cup (4 oz.) shredded process American cheese

1 Preheat oven to 350°F. Grease two 2-quart rectangular baking dishes; set aside. In an extra-large skillet cook meat and onion until meat is brown and onion is tender, stirring to break up meat. Drain off fat. Add the salt and pepper. Stir in beans and soup. Divide mixture between prepared baking dishes.

2 Spoon potatoes in mounds on top of bean mixture (or, if desired, pipe potatoes using a pastry bag and a large star tip). Sprinkle cheese over the potatoes.

3 Bake, uncovered, for 30 to 35 minutes or until mixture is bubbly and cheese begins to brown.

Makes 12 servings

Per serving: 376 cal., 16 g total fat (8 g sat. fat), 80 mg chol., 796 mg sodium, 34 g carbo., 4 g fiber, 23 g pro.

Grandma's Spaghetti Casserole

This old-fashioned supper dish is what Grandma would serve. It's welcoming, warm, and wonderful.

Prep: 35 minutes   **Bake:** 45 minutes   **Oven:** 350°F

16   oz. dried spaghetti
 1   lb. ground beef
 1   cup chopped onion
 1   cup chopped green sweet pepper
 2   14.5-oz. cans diced tomatoes, undrained
 2   10.75-oz. cans condensed tomato soup
 1   tsp. black pepper
 4   cups (16 oz.) shredded cheddar cheese
 8   slices bacon, crisp-cooked, drained, and crumbled

1 Preheat oven to 350°F. Cook spaghetti according to package directions; drain. Set aside. Grease two 2-quart casseroles.

2 Meanwhile, in an extra-large skillet cook ground beef, onion, and sweet pepper over medium heat until meat is brown, stirring to break up meat; drain off fat. Stir in undrained tomatoes, soup, and black pepper. Bring just to boiling. Add half of the shredded cheese, stirring until melted.

3 Toss meat mixture and bacon with cooked spaghetti. Divide mixture between prepared casseroles. Cover casseroles.

4 Bake for 30 minutes. Uncover; sprinkle with the remaining cheese. Bake, uncovered, about 15 minutes more or until bubbly and heated through.

Makes 8 servings.

Per serving: 675 cal., 31 g total fat (16 g sat. fat), 100 mg chol., 1,007 mg sodium, 61 g carbo., 3 g fiber, 35 g pro.

Mexicali Hamburger Casserole

Spoon into this colorful casserole for a full-fledged fiesta baked beneath a tender crust of corn bread.

Prep: 30 minutes   **Bake:** 30 minutes   **Stand:** 5 minutes   **Oven:** 350°F

- 3 lb. lean ground beef
- 2 14.5-oz. cans diced tomatoes with chili spices, undrained
- 3 cups frozen whole kernel corn, thawed
- 1¼ cups finely shredded Mexican cheese blend
- 1 cup all-purpose flour
- 1 cup yellow cornmeal
- 2 Tbsp. sugar
- 2½ tsp. baking powder
- 1 tsp. salt
- 2 eggs, beaten
- 1⅓ cups milk
- ¼ cup vegetable oil
- 2 cups red grape tomatoes, halved
- ½ cup coarsely snipped fresh cilantro
- ⅔ cup pitted green olives, halved (optional)

1 Preheat oven to 350°F. Grease two 2-quart baking dishes; set aside. In an extra-large skillet cook ground beef until brown, stirring to break up meat; drain off fat. Stir in undrained tomatoes and two-thirds of the corn; heat through. Divide mixture between prepared baking dishes. Sprinkle with 1 cup of the cheese.

2 For corn bread topping, in a large bowl combine flour, cornmeal, sugar, baking powder, and salt. In a bowl combine eggs, milk, and oil. Stir into flour mixture until all is moistened. Evenly spread topping on meat mixture. Sprinkle the remaining cheese.

3 Bake, uncovered, about 30 minutes or until topping is set. Let stand for 5 minutes.

4 Meanwhile, in a bowl combine the remaining corn, the tomatoes, cilantro, and, if desired, olives. Serve with casserole.

Makes 12 servings

Per serving: 506 cal., 27 g total fat (10 g sat. fat), 125 mg chol., 603 mg sodium, 38 g carbo., 2 g fiber, 30 g pro.

Stuffed Cabbage Rolls

These plump cabbage rolls are nestled on a bed of sauerkraut. Not fond of sauerkraut? Just omit the kraut layer in the bottom of the dish.

Prep: 50 minutes   **Bake:** 40 minutes   **Oven:** 350°F

16	medium to large cabbage leaves
1½	lb. lean ground beef
1	cup chopped onion
2	cups cooked white rice
2	slightly beaten eggs
¼	cup snipped fresh parsley
½	tsp. salt
1	32-oz. jar sauerkraut, rinsed and well drained
1	15-oz. can tomato sauce
¼	cup water
¼	cup packed brown sugar
4	tsp. lemon juice
	Dash ground allspice or ground cloves

1 Trim veins from cabbage leaves. Immerse leaves, four at a time, into boiling water. Cook for 2 to 3 minutes or until leaves are just limp. Carefully remove leaves with tongs or a slotted spoon; drain well.

2 Meanwhile, for filling, in a large skillet cook ground beef and onion until meat is brown; drain off fat. In a medium bowl combine cooked beef mixture, rice, eggs, parsley, and salt.

3 Preheat oven to 350°F. Grease two 2-quart rectangular or square baking dishes; divide sauerkraut evenly between the two dishes.

4 Place about ⅓ cup of the filling in the center of each cabbage leaf; fold in sides. Starting at an unfolded edge, carefully roll each leaf, making sure folded sides are tucked into the roll. Arrange cabbage rolls on sauerkraut in baking dishes.

5 For sauce, stir together the tomato sauce, water, brown sugar, lemon juice, and allspice; pour sauce over cabbage rolls. Bake, covered, about 40 minutes or until heated through.

Makes 8 servings

Per serving: 285 cal., 10 g total fat (4 g sat. fat), 107 mg chol., 1,242 mg sodium, 29 g carbo., 6 g fiber, 19 g pro.

To tote: *Transport in an insulated carrier.*

Beefy Vegetables and Noodles

Fresh corn, sweet pepper, pimiento, onion, and mushrooms add interest and vitamins to this creamy dish.

Prep: 35 minutes **Bake:** 30 minutes **Oven:** 350°F

- 2 8-oz. pkgs. extra-wide noodles
- 2 lb. lean ground beef or ground raw turkey
- 1½ cups coarsely chopped green sweet pepper
- 1 cup chopped onion
- 1 16-oz. pkg. frozen whole kernel corn or 4 fresh ears of corn, cooked and cut off the cob
- 2 10.75-oz. cans condensed golden mushroom soup
- 2 cups chopped fresh mushrooms
- 1 8-oz. pkg. cream cheese, cut up
- ⅔ cup milk
- 1 4-oz. jar diced pimiento, drained
- 1 tsp. salt
- 1 tsp. dried marjoram, crushed
- ½ tsp. black pepper

1 Preheat oven to 350°F. Cook noodles according to package directions. Drain; rinse and drain again.

2 Meanwhile, in a 4-quart Dutch oven cook ground beef, sweet pepper, and onion until meat is brown and vegetables are tender; drain off fat. Stir in corn, soup, mushrooms, cream cheese, milk, pimiento, salt, marjoram, and black pepper. Heat and stir until cream cheese melts. Gently stir in cooked noodles.

3 Divide ground beef mixture between two ungreased 2-quart rectangular baking dishes. Bake, covered, for 30 to 35 minutes or until heated through.

Makes 12 servings

Per serving: 416 cal., 18 g total fat (8 g sat. fat), 107 mg chol., 688 mg sodium, 41 g carbo., 3 g fiber, 23 g pro.

To tote: *Transport in an insulated carrier.*

Eggplant and Beef Casserole

Eggplant, ground beef, Italian seasoning, and a combination of mozzarella and Parmesan cheeses join forces in this delicious dinner in a dish.

Prep: 50 minutes   **Bake:** 30 minutes   **Stand:** 10 minutes   **Oven:** 350°F

- ¾   cup milk
- 1   beaten egg
- ¾   cup all-purpose flour
- ½   tsp. salt
- ¼   tsp. black pepper
- 1   1½-pound eggplant, peeled and sliced ½ inch thick
- 3   Tbsp. vegetable oil
- 1   lb. lean ground beef
- 1   cup chopped green sweet pepper
- ¾   cup chopped onion
- 1   15-oz. can tomato sauce
- 1   8-oz. can tomato sauce
- 1½   tsp. dried Italian seasoning, crushed
- 2   cups (8 oz.) shredded Italian cheese blend

1 Grease a 3-quart rectangular baking dish; set dish aside. In a small bowl combine milk and egg. In a shallow dish combine flour, salt, and pepper.

2 Dip eggplant slices in egg mixture; coat with flour mixture. In an extra-large skillet cook eggplant slices, several at a time, in hot oil for 2 minutes on each side or until golden. Repeat with remaining eggplant slices, adding more oil if necessary. Drain on paper towels.

3 Preheat oven to 350°F. In a large skillet cook ground beef, sweet pepper, and onion until meat is brown; drain off fat. Stir in tomato sauce and Italian seasoning.

4 Layer half of the eggplant slices in the prepared baking dish, cutting slices to fit. Spread with half of the meat mixture; sprinkle with half of the cheese. Repeat layers. Bake, covered, for 20 minutes. Uncover and bake for 10 to 15 minutes more or until heated through. Let stand for 10 minutes before serving (if toting, see note).

Makes 8 servings

Per serving: 340 cal., 19 g total fat (7 g sat. fat), 84 mg chol., 796 mg sodium, 23 g carbo., 4 g fiber, 22 g pro.

To tote: *Do not let stand after baking. Cover tightly. Transport in an insulated carrier.*

Upside-Down Pizza Casse

Refrigerated biscuits bake to golden p
top of this cheesy-rich five-ingredient filling.

Prep: 25 minutes   **Bake:** 15 minutes   **Oven:** 400°F

- 3   lb. lean ground beef
- 2   15-oz. cans Italian-style tomato sauce
- 2   4-oz. cans (drained weight) sliced mushrooms, drained
- ½   cup sliced pitted ripe olives (optional)
- 2   to 3 cups (8 to 12 oz.) shredded mozzarella cheese
- 2   10-oz. pkg. (10 biscuits each) refrigerated biscuits

1 Preheat oven to 400°F. In an extra-large skillet cook ground beef until brown, stirring to break up meat. Drain off fat. Stir in tomato sauce, mushrooms, and, if desired, olives. Heat through. Divide mixture between two 2-quart rectangular baking dishes. Sprinkle with cheese.

2 Flatten each biscuit with your hands. Arrange the biscuits on top of cheese. Bake for 15 to 17 minutes or until biscuits are golden.

Makes 10 servings

Per serving: 507 cal., 26 g total fat (10 g sat. fat), 103 mg chol., 1,251 mg sodium, 33 g carbo., 3 g fiber, 35 g pro.

Chili-Pasta Skillet

In this recipe the macaroni cooks along with the other ingredients, saving busy cooks the time and trouble of precooking and draining the pasta.

Prep: 15 minutes   **Cook:** 20 minutes   **Stand:** 2 minutes

- 2 lb. ground beef
- 1½ cups chopped onion
- 2 15.5-oz. cans red kidney beans, rinsed and drained
- 2 14.5-oz. cans diced tomatoes, undrained
- 1 15-oz. can tomato sauce
- 2 4-oz. cans diced green chile peppers, drained
- 1 cup (4 oz.) dried elbow macaroni
- 4 to 6 tsp. chili powder
- 1 tsp. garlic salt
- 1 cup (4 oz.) shredded Monterey Jack cheese or cheddar cheese

1 In an extra-large skillet cook meat and onion until meat is brown and onion is tender, stirring to break up meat. Drain off fat.

2 Stir in beans, undrained tomatoes, tomato sauce, chile peppers, uncooked macaroni, chili powder, and garlic salt. Bring to boiling; reduce heat. Simmer, covered, about 20 minutes or until macaroni is tender, stirring often. Remove skillet from heat; sprinkle mixture with cheese. Cover and let stand about 2 minutes or until cheese is melted.

Makes 12 servings

Per serving: 311 cal., 13 g total fat (5 g sat. fat), 56 mg chol., 634 mg sodium, 27 g carbo., 5 g fiber, 24 g pro.

Easy Shepherd's Pie

*Talk about a package deal! Every ma
ingredient—from beef and sauce to potatoes
and cheese—comes from a package.*

Prep: 20 minutes   **Bake:** 20 minutes   **Stand:** 10 minutes   **Oven:** 375°F

2   17-oz. pkg. refrigerated
    cooked beef tips with
    gravy

4   cups frozen mixed
    vegetable blend (any
    combination)

2   10.75-oz. cans condensed
    tomato bisque soup

2   Tbsp. Worcestershire
    sauce

2   tsp. dried minced onion

1   tsp. dried thyme, crushed

¼   tsp. black pepper

1   20-oz. pkg. refrigerated
    mashed potatoes

1   cup (4 oz.) shredded
    cheddar cheese

1 Preheat oven to 375°F. Lightly grease a 3-quart rectangular baking dish. In a large saucepan combine beef tips with gravy, frozen vegetables, soup, Worcestershire sauce, onion, thyme, and pepper. Bring to boiling over medium heat, stirring occasionally. Transfer mixture to the prepared baking dish.

2 Stir mashed potatoes to soften. Spoon potatoes in eight mounds on meat mixture. Sprinkle with cheese.

3 Bake, uncovered, for 20 to 25 minutes or until heated through. Let stand for 10 minutes before serving.

Makes 8 servings

Per serving: 438 cal., 15 g total fat (6 g sat. fat), 64 mg chol., 1,570 mg sodium, 49 g carbo., 5 g fiber, 27 g pro.

Mexican-Style Moussaka

To hard-cook eggs, place in a saucepan and cover with cold water. Bring to boiling; boil 1 minute. Cover pan, remove from heat, and allow to stand 15 minutes. Cool eggs quickly in ice water; peel.

Prep: 25 minutes   **Bake:** 30 minutes   **Stand:** 10 minutes   **Oven:** 350°F

- 2 lb. lean ground beef
- 2 cups chopped onion
- 2 Tbsp. all-purpose flour
- 4 tsp. chili powder
- 1 tsp. ground cumin
- 1 tsp. salt
- ½ tsp. black pepper
- 4 hard-cooked eggs, coarsely chopped
- 2 eggs, slightly beaten
- 1 14.75-oz. can cream-style corn

1 Preheat oven to 350°F. In an extra-large skillet cook ground beef and onion until meat is brown and onion is tender, stirring to break up meat; drain off fat. Stir flour, chili powder, cumin, half of the salt, and the pepper into meat mixture. Cook and stir for 1 minute. Stir in hard-cooked eggs. Transfer mixture to a 3-quart rectangular baking dish.

2 In a bowl combine slightly beaten eggs, corn, and the remaining salt; spoon over meat mixture.

3 Bake, uncovered, about 30 minutes or just until center is set. Let stand for 10 minutes before serving.

Makes 8 servings

Per serving: 367 cal., 21 g total fat (8 g sat. fat), 236 mg chol., 600 mg sodium, 17 g carbo., 2 g fiber, 28 g pro.

Pioneer Beans and Beef

If you like barbecued beans, you'll love this dish. Three types of beans, beef, bacon, molasses, and brown sugar combine for a tasty dish.

Prep: 20 minutes   **Bake:** 1 hour   **Oven:** 350°F

- 1 lb. ground beef
- 4 slices bacon, chopped
- ½ cup chopped onion
- 1 15-oz. can red kidney beans, rinsed and drained
- 1 15-oz. can butter beans, rinsed and drained
- 1 15-oz. can pork and beans in tomato sauce, undrained
- 1 cup ketchup
- ⅓ cup packed brown sugar
- ¼ cup mild-flavor molasses
- 1 Tbsp. vinegar
- 1 Tbsp. prepared mustard

1 Preheat oven to 350°F. In a large skillet cook the ground beef, bacon, and onion until meat is brown and onion is tender; drain off fat. Stir in kidney beans, butter beans, pork and beans, ketchup, brown sugar, molasses, vinegar, and mustard.

2 Transfer to a 2- to 2½-quart casserole. Bake, covered, for 30 minutes. Uncover and bake for 30 minutes more.

Makes 8 servings

Per serving: 357 cal., 9 g total fat (4 g sat. fat), 42 mg chol., 982 mg sodium, 51 g carbo., 8 g fiber, 22 g pro.

Slow cooker directions: *Prepare as directed, except transfer meat and bean mixture to a 3½- or 4-quart slow cooker. Cover and cook on low-heat setting for 5 to 6 hours or on high-heat setting for 2½ to 3 hours.*

To tote: *Cover tightly. Transport in an insulated carrier. (Or, if desired, transport crockery cooker in an insulated carrier.)*

Norwegian Meatballs

These magnificent meatballs—bathed in a sauce infused with the sweet, warm spiciness of nutmeg—are divine.

Prep: 35 minutes   **Bake:** 30 minutes   **Oven:** 350°F

4 eggs, beaten

2½ cups milk

1⅓ cups (about 36 crackers) crushed saltine crackers

⅔ cup finely chopped onion

1 tsp. celery salt

1 tsp. ground nutmeg

1 tsp. black pepper

4 lb. lean ground beef

2 10.75-oz. cans condensed cream of mushroom soup

Hot cooked noodles (optional)

Peas (optional)

1 Preheat oven to 350°F. Grease two 3-quart rectangular baking dishes; set aside. In a bowl combine eggs and 1 cup of the milk. Stir in crushed crackers, onion, celery salt, half of the nutmeg, and the pepper. Add ground beef; mix well. Shape mixture into 40 meatballs. Arrange meatballs in prepared baking dish. Bake, uncovered, about 30 minutes or until the internal temperature of each meatball registers 160°F.

2 For sauce, in a saucepan combine soup, the remaining milk, and the remaining nutmeg. Cook and stir over medium heat until heated through. Serve sauce over meatballs. If desired, serve with noodles and peas.

Makes 10 or 12 servings

Per serving: 469 cal., 26 g total fat (10 g sat. fat), 204 mg chol., 842 mg sodium, 17 g carbo., 1 g fiber, 39 g pro.

Cheeseburger and Fries Casserole

If kids were in charge of family nutrition, this easy-going recipe would be on the menu every night of the week.

Prep: 20 minutes   **Bake:** 45 minutes   **Oven:** 350°F

- 4 lb. lean ground beef
- 2 10.75-oz. cans condensed golden mushroom soup
- 2 10.75-oz. cans condensed cheddar cheese soup
- 2 20-oz. pkg. frozen french-fried crinkle-cut potatoes

   Toppings (such as ketchup, pickles, mustard, and chopped tomato) (optional)

1 Preheat oven to 350°F. In an extra-large skillet cook half of the ground beef until brown, stirring to break up meat. Drain off fat; spoon meat into a 3-quart rectangular baking dish. Repeat with remaining ground beef, using another 3-quart rectangular baking dish. In a bowl combine golden mushroom soup and cheddar cheese soup. Spread over the meat. Sprinkle the potatoes on top of soup.

2 Bake, uncovered, for 45 to 55 minutes or until the fries are golden. If desired, serve with toppings.

Makes 16 servings

Per serving: 348 cal., 18 g total fat (6 g sat. fat), 78 mg chol., 654 mg sodium, 24 g carbo., 2 g fiber, 24 g pro.

Italian Crescent Casserole

Crescent rolls pinch hit for the crust, cutting the time spent in the kitchen. Use your favorite brand of spaghetti or pasta sauce (including chunky vegetables, if you like) for a tailored dish.

Prep: 25 minutes   **Bake:** 20 minutes   **Oven:** 375°F

- 2 lb. lean ground beef
- ½ cup chopped onion
- 2 cups bottled spaghetti or pasta sauce
- 3 cups (12 oz.) shredded mozzarella or Monterey Jack cheese
- 1 8-oz. carton sour cream
- 1 8-oz. pkg. (8) refrigerated crescent rolls
- 2 Tbsp. butter or margarine, melted
- ½ cup grated Parmesan cheese

1 Preheat oven to 375°F. In an extra-large skillet cook ground beef and onion until meat is brown; drain off fat. Stir in spaghetti sauce; heat through. Spread meat mixture in an ungreased 3-quart rectangular baking dish.

2 Meanwhile, combine mozzarella cheese and sour cream; spoon over meat mixture in baking dish.

3 Unroll crescent rolls, but do not separate into triangles. On a lightly floured surface, press dough edges together and roll out slightly to fit dish. Place dough over the cheese layer. Brush with melted butter and sprinkle with Parmesan cheese. Bake, uncovered, for 20 to 25 minutes or until top is deep golden brown.

Makes 12 servings

Per serving: 360 cal., 23 g total fat (11 g sat. fat), 81 mg chol., 593 mg sodium, 14 g carbo., 0 g fiber, 25 g pro.

To tote: *Cover tightly. Transport in an insulated carrier.*

Pizza in a Bowl

No crust required. Simply spoon this pasta mixture, which boasts all the typical pizza toppers, into a bowl to serve.

Prep: 30 minutes   **Bake:** 35 minutes   **Oven:** 350°F

- 2   cups dried rotini
- 1   3½-oz. pkg. thinly sliced pepperoni
- 1   pound lean ground beef
- ⅓   cup finely chopped onion
- 1   15-oz. can pizza sauce
- 1   8-oz. can tomato sauce
- 1   6-oz. can tomato paste
- ½   tsp. sugar
- ¼   tsp. garlic salt or onion salt
- ⅛   tsp. black pepper
- 2   cups (8 oz.) shredded mozzarella cheese
- 2   Tbsp. grated Parmesan cheese

1 Cook pasta according to package directions, except omit salt; drain well. Meanwhile, cut half of the pepperoni slices into quarters; set aside.

2 Preheat oven to 350°F. In a large skillet cook ground beef and onion until meat is brown and onion is tender; drain off fat. Stir in pizza sauce, tomato sauce, tomato paste, sugar, garlic salt, and pepper. Stir in the cooked rotini and quartered pepperoni slices.

3 Spoon half of the rotini mixture into a 2-quart casserole; sprinkle with half of the mozzarella cheese. Repeat layers. Top with Parmesan cheese and remaining pepperoni slices. Bake, uncovered, for 35 to 40 minutes or until heated through.

Makes 6 servings

Per serving: 521 cal., 21 g total fat (10 g sat. fat), 84 mg chol., 1,184 mg sodium, 45 g carbo., 3 g fiber, 35 g pro.

To tote: *Cover tightly. Transport in an insulated carrier.*

Bean and Beef Enchilada Casserole

Consider this hearty casserole as comfort food with a south-of-the-border twist. It is the perfect dish to come home to after a long day.

Prep: 35 minutes   **Bake:** 40 minutes   **Oven:** 350°F

- 12   oz. lean ground beef
- ¾   cup chopped onion
- 1½   tsp. chili powder
- ¾   tsp. ground cumin
- 2   15-oz. cans pinto beans, rinsed and drained
- 2   4-oz. cans diced green chile peppers, undrained
- 1½   cups sour cream
- 3   Tbsp. all-purpose flour
- ½   tsp. garlic powder
- 12   6-inch corn tortillas
- 2   10-oz. cans enchilada sauce
- 1   cup (4 oz.) shredded cheddar cheese

  Fresh cilantro and fresh chile peppers (optional)

1 Preheat oven to 350°F. In a large skillet cook the ground beef and onion until meat is brown and onion is tender; drain off fat. Stir in chili powder and cumin; cook and stir 1 minute more. Stir pinto beans and undrained chile peppers into meat mixture; set aside. In a small bowl stir together sour cream, flour, and garlic powder; set aside.

2 Place half of the tortillas in the bottom of a lightly greased 3-quart rectangular baking dish, cutting to fit and overlapping as necessary. Top with half of the meat mixture, half of the sour cream mixture, and half of the enchilada sauce. Repeat layers.

3 Bake, covered, for 35 to 40 minutes or until heated through. Uncover and sprinkle with cheese. Bake about 5 minutes more or until cheese is melted. If desired, garnish with cilantro and fresh chile peppers.

Makes 12 servings

Per serving: 304 cal., 14 g total fat (7 g sat. fat), 38 mg chol., 682 mg sodium, 32 g carbo., 6 g fiber, 15 g pro.

To tote: *Cover tightly. Transport in an insulated carrier. If desired, transport cilantro and chile peppers in an airtight container.*

Cheesy Pasta-Beef Bake

Sour cream, cream cheese, and cheddar cheese create a richly flavored sauce in this beefy pasta dish. The beef, pasta, and white sauce form distinct layers when served.

Prep: 30 minutes   **Bake:** 30 minutes   **Oven:** 350°F

- 16 oz. (about 5½ cups) dried rotini or elbow macaroni
- 2 lb. lean ground beef
- 2 15-oz. cans Italian-style tomato sauce
- 2 8-oz. containers sour cream chive dip
- 6 oz. cream cheese, softened
- ¼ cup milk
- 1½ cups (6 oz.) shredded cheddar cheese and/or mozzarella cheese
- ¼ cup sliced green onions (optional)

1 Preheat oven to 350°F. Grease two 2-quart rectangular baking dishes; set dishes aside. Cook rotini according to package directions; drain. Meanwhile, in a large skillet cook ground beef until brown; drain off fat. Stir in tomato sauce. Bring to boiling; reduce heat. Simmer, uncovered, for 15 minutes, stirring occasionally.

2 In a small bowl combine dip, cream cheese, and milk. Layer beef mixture, cooked pasta, and dip mixture in prepared baking dishes.

3 Bake, covered, for 15 minutes. Uncover and sprinkle with cheese. Bake, uncovered, for 15 minutes more. If desired, top with green onions.

Makes 16 servings

Per serving: 354 cal., 19 g total fat (10 g sat. fat), 71 mg chol., 613 mg sodium, 28 g carbo., 2 g fiber, 19 g pro.

To tote: *Cover tightly. Transport in an insulated carrier. If desired, transport green onions in an insulated cooler with ice packs.*

Italian Beef Sandwiches

The meat for these sandwiches is cooked in a slow cooker. Let it cook all day for an evening gathering. For a large crowd, use small dinner rolls to make the meat go further.

Prep: 10 minutes   **Cook:** 10 hours (low) or 5 hours (high)

1	4-lb. boneless beef sirloin or rump roast, cut into 2- to 3-inch pieces
½	cup water
1	0.7-oz. envelope Italian dry salad dressing mix
2	tsp. Italian seasoning, crushed
½	to 1 tsp. crushed red pepper
½	tsp. garlic powder
12	kaiser rolls or other sandwich rolls, split
	Roasted red sweet pepper strips (optional)

1 Place beef in a 3½-, 4-, or 5-quart slow cooker. Stir together water, salad dressing mix, Italian seasoning, crushed red pepper, and garlic powder; pour over beef in slow cooker. Cover and cook on low-heat setting for 10 to 12 hours or on high-heat setting for 5 to 6 hours.

2 Remove meat with a slotted spoon. Using two forks, shred the meat. Serve meat on rolls. Drizzle each sandwich with some of the juices to moisten. If desired, top each sandwich with roasted red pepper strips.

Makes 12 sandwiches

Per sandwich: 361 cal., 8 g total fat (2 g sat. fat), 91 mg chol., 598 mg sodium, 31 g carbo., 1 g fiber, 38 g pro.

To tote: *Return shredded meat to slow cooker. Transport slow cooker in an insulated carrier. (Or, if desired, transfer shredded meat and juices to a serving dish. Cover tightly. Transport in an insulated carrier.) If desired, transport roasted red pepper strips in an airtight container. Serve meat with a slotted spoon.*

Hearty Chili

To add a riot of color and lots of vita[...] slow cooker stunner, chop up a trio o[...] and green sweet peppers.

Prep: 15 minutes   **Cook:** 10 hours (low) or 5 hours (high)

2 lb. boneless beef round steak or boneless pork shoulder

2 cups chopped onion

1½ cups chopped yellow, red, and/or green sweet peppers

2 15-oz. cans chili beans with chili gravy

2 14.5-oz. cans stewed tomatoes, undrained and cut up

1 15.5-oz. can red kidney beans or pinto beans, rinsed and drained

1 cup beer or beef broth

2 to 3 tsp. chopped canned chipotle chile peppers in adobo sauce (see note, page 15)

2 tsp. garlic salt

2 tsp. ground cumin

1 tsp. dried oregano, crushed

Shredded cheddar cheese, chopped onion, and/or sour cream (optional)

1 Trim meat and cut into ½-inch cubes. In a 5½- to 6-quart slow cooker combine meat, onion, sweet peppers, chili beans in chili gravy, undrained tomatoes, kidney beans, beer, chile peppers, garlic salt, cumin, and oregano.

2 Cover and cook on low-heat setting for 10 to 12 hours or on high-heat setting for 5 to 6 hours. Spoon off fat. If desired, serve with cheese, onion, and/or sour cream.

Makes 10 to 12 servings

Per serving: 296 cal., 5 g total fat (1 g sat. fat), 52 mg chol., 821 mg sodium, 34 g carbo., 8 g fiber, 29 g pro.

Down-South Barbecue Sandwiches

This recipe features both beef and pork, which are cooked to tender perfection and shredded. It easily feeds a crowd of hungry tailgaters.

Prep: 15 minutes   **Cook:** 2½ hours

- 1   cup water
- 1   6-oz. can tomato paste
- ½   cup packed brown sugar
- ¼   cup cider vinegar
- 2   Tbsp. chili powder
- 2   tsp. Worcestershire sauce
- 1   tsp. dry mustard
- 1½   lb. boneless beef chuck roast
- 1½   lb. boneless pork shoulder roast
- 16   hamburger buns, split and toasted

1 For sauce, in a 4-quart Dutch oven combine water, tomato paste, brown sugar, vinegar, chili powder, Worcestershire sauce, and dry mustard. Add beef and pork roasts to sauce, cutting meat to fit in Dutch oven if necessary.

2 Bring to boiling; reduce heat. Simmer, covered, about 2½ hours or until meat is very tender, stirring occasionally.

3 Remove meat from pan, reserving sauce in Dutch oven. Shred meat with two forks. Stir shredded meat into sauce in Dutch oven. Serve meat mixture on buns.

Makes 16 sandwiches

Per sandwich: 286 cal., 8 g total fat (3 g sat. fat), 56 mg chol., 330 mg sodium, 31 g carbo., 2 g fiber, 21 g pro.

Slow cooker directions: *Use ingredient amounts listed, except reduce water in sauce to ¼ cup. Place beef and pork roasts in a 3½- or 4-quart slow cooker, cutting meat to fit if necessary. Pour sauce over meat in cooker. Cover and cook on low-heat setting for 10 to 12 hours or on high-heat setting for 5 to 6 hours. Remove meat from slow cooker, reserving sauce. Shred meat with two forks. Stir together shredded meat and reserved sauce in cooker.*

To tote: *Transfer meat mixture to serving dish. Cover tightly. Transport in an insulated carrier. (Or, if desired, transport slow cooker in an insulated carrier.)*

Zucchini-Pork Chop Supper

Gardeners who are familiar with the abundance of late-summer zucchini will relish this recipe. It is a tasty way to serve this versatile veggie.

Prep: 35 minutes   **Bake:** 50 minutes   **Oven:** 350°F

2	14-oz. pkg. herb-seasoned stuffing croutons
½	cup butter or margarine, melted
8	cups coarsely chopped zucchini
2	10.75-oz. cans condensed cream of celery soup
1	16-oz. carton light sour cream
1½	cups milk
1	cup shredded carrot
2	Tbsp. snipped fresh parsley
½	to 1 tsp. black pepper
12	bone-in pork loin chops cut ¾ inch thick

1 Preheat oven to 350°F. Grease two 3-quart rectangular baking dishes; set aside. In a large bowl combine 15 cups of the croutons and the melted butter; toss gently to coat. Spread one-fourth of the buttered croutons into each baking dish. Set aside.

2 In another large bowl combine zucchini, soup, sour cream, two-thirds of the milk, the carrot, parsley, and pepper. Spoon evenly over buttered croutons in baking dishes. Sprinkle with the remaining buttered croutons.

3 Pour the remaining milk into a shallow dish. Coarsely crush the remaining croutons; place in another shallow dish. Trim fat from chops. Dip chops into milk, then into crushed croutons, turning to coat on both sides. Place chops on top of layers in baking dishes. Sprinkle with any remaining crushed croutons.

4 Bake, uncovered, for 50 to 60 minutes or until chops are slightly pink in center and juices run clear (160°F).

Makes 12 servings.

Per serving: 639 cal., 24 g total fat (10 g sat. fat), 130 mg chol., 1,417 mg sodium, 57 g carbo., 4 g fiber, 46 g pro.

Southwest Spaghetti Pie

This pie will be a hit at any potluck with kids present! Cooked spaghetti makes up the crust. The topping is loaded with cheese, tomato sauce, and ground pork.

Prep: 40 minutes   **Bake:** 10 minutes   **Stand:** 5 minutes   **Oven:** 425°F

8   oz. dried spaghetti
½   cup milk
1   egg
1   lb. ground pork
1   cup chopped onion
¾   cup chopped green sweet pepper
1   clove garlic, minced
1   Tbsp. chili powder
½   tsp. salt
½   tsp. ground cumin
½   tsp. dried oregano, crushed
¼   tsp. black pepper
1   15-oz. can tomato sauce
1   cup (4 oz.) shredded Monterey Jack cheese with jalapeño peppers
1   cup (4 oz.) shredded cheddar cheese

1 Preheat oven to 425°F. Cook spaghetti according to package directions; drain well. Return to pan. Combine milk and egg; stir into hot pasta. Transfer to a buttered 3-quart rectangular baking dish (there will be some liquid).

2 Meanwhile, in a large skillet cook pork, onion, sweet pepper, and garlic until meat is brown; drain off fat. Stir in chili powder, salt, cumin, oregano, and black pepper. Cook and stir for 2 minutes. Stir in tomato sauce. Bring to boiling; reduce heat. Simmer, uncovered, for 2 minutes more. Spoon over pasta in baking dish. Sprinkle with cheeses.

3 Bake, uncovered, about 10 minutes or until bubbly around the edges. Let stand for 5 minutes before serving (if toting, see note).

Makes 8 servings

Per serving: 330 cal., 15 g total fat (8 g sat. fat), 84 mg chol., 621 mg sodium, 29 g carbo., 2 g fiber, 20 g pro.

To tote: *Do not let stand after baking. Cover tightly. Transport in an insulated carrier.*

Santa Fe Pork Pie

In New Mexico, the residents love their green chiles and use them often. This simple, scrumptious pie showcases the subtle heat of green chiles.

Prep: 35 minutes   **Bake:** 15 minutes   **Oven:** 425°F

2⅔   cups chicken broth

6   medium potatoes, peeled and cut into ½-inch cubes

1   cup sliced celery

8   cloves garlic, minced

4   tsp. chili powder

2   tsp. dried thyme, crushed

2   lb. boneless pork loin, cut into ¾-inch cubes

¼   cup vegetable oil

2   4-oz. cans diced green chile peppers, drained

8   tsp. dried cilantro, crushed

2   7.5-oz. pkgs. refrigerated biscuits

Sour cream (optional)

1 Preheat oven to 425°F. In a saucepan combine broth, potatoes, celery, and garlic. Bring to boiling; reduce heat. Simmer, covered, for 8 to 10 minutes or until potatoes are nearly tender. Do not drain.

2 Meanwhile, for filling, in a bowl combine chili powder and thyme. Add pork cubes; toss to coat. In an extra-large skillet heat oil over medium heat. Add half of the pork; cook in hot oil for 4 to 5 minutes or until no longer pink. Using a slotted spoon; remove meat from skillet; set aside. Repeat with remaining meat; drain. Return all meat to skillet. Add potato mixture, chile peppers, and cilantro. Bring to boiling. Divide mixture between two 2-quart casseroles.

3 Snip each biscuit into 4 pieces; arrange on top of hot mixture. Bake, uncovered, about 15 minutes or until biscuits are golden. If desired, top with sour cream.

Makes 12 servings

Per serving: 240 cal., 10 g total fat (2 g sat. fat), 45 mg chol., 388 mg sodium, 18 g carbo., 2 g fiber, 19 g pro.

Pork Soft Shell Tacos

No need for charcoal or matches—chipotle chile powder is all you'll need to imbue this skillet-cooked pork with smoky flavor.

Start to Finish: 25 minutes

- 8   ounces boneless pork loin
- 2   teaspoons vegetable oil
- ¼   cup light sour cream
- ¼   teaspoon chipotle chili powder, crushed dried chipotle chile pepper, or chili powder
- 4   6-inch flour tortillas, warmed if desired*
- ½   cup shredded lettuce
- ½   cup diced tomato (1 medium)
- ½   cup shredded reduced-fat cheddar cheese (2 ounces)
       Salsa

1 If desired, partially freeze meat for easier slicing. Trim fat from meat. Thinly slice meat across the grain into bite-size strips. In a large skillet cook meat in hot oil over medium-high heat until brown; set aside.

2 In a small bowl combine sour cream and chipotle chili powder, chipotle pepper, or chili powder; set aside.

3 Spoon one-quarter of the meat onto each tortilla just below the center. Top meat with lettuce, tomato, and cheese. Fold top half of each tortilla over filling. Serve with sour cream mixture and salsa.

Makes 4 servings

Per serving: 240 cal., 11 g total fat (4 g sat. fat), 48 mg chol., 263 mg sodium, 14 g carbo., 1 g fiber, 19 g pro.

- -

*Note: *To warm tortillas, preheat oven to 350°F. Wrap tortillas in foil. Bake for 10 to 15 minutes or until warmed.*

Potato-Ham Bake

To trim asparagus, grasp a spear with one hand on the tapered end and one on the stem end. Bend until the stem breaks. The spear will naturally break to separate tender spear from tough stem.

Prep: 30 minutes   **Bake:** 30 minutes   **Stand:** 5 minutes   **Oven:** 400°F

2 lb. Yukon gold potatoes, sliced

2 8-oz. tubs light cream cheese spread with chive and onion

1½ cups milk

½ cup (2 oz.) finely shredded Parmesan cheese

½ tsp. black pepper

2 Tbsp. snipped fresh tarragon

1 lb. cooked boneless ham, cut in bite-size pieces

2 lb. fresh asparagus spears, trimmed and cut in 2- to 3-inch pieces

Tarragon sprigs (optional)

1 Preheat oven to 400°F. In a covered saucepan cook potatoes in small amount of lightly salted boiling water for 5 to 7 minute or just until tender. Drain;. Remove potatoes from saucepan; set aside.

2 For sauce, in same saucepan combine cream cheese, milk, half of the Parmesan cheese, and the pepper. Whisk over low heat until mixture is smooth and cheese is melted. Remove from heat; stir in tarragon.

3 Layer potatoes, ham, asparagus, and sauce in 3-quart rectangular baking dish. Cover with foil.

4 Bake for 20 minutes. Uncover; sprinkle with the remaining Parmesan cheese. Bake for 10 to 12 minutes or until heated through. Let stand for 5 minutes before serving. If desired, top with tarragon sprigs.

Makes 8 servings

Per serving: 346 cal., 16 g total fat (9 g sat. fat), 67 mg chol., 1,162 mg sodium, 30 g carbo., 5 g fiber, 22 g pro.

Spinach and Ham Lasagna

Deviate from the traditional red-sauced lasagna. This luscious lasagna is layered with spinach, ham, cheese, and a lightened cream sauce. Ham adds a tasty smoky flavor.

Prep: 40 minutes   **Bake:** 30 minutes   **Stand:** 10 minutes   **Oven:** 375°F

8	dried lasagna noodles
3	cups milk
⅓	cup chopped onion
¼	cup cornstarch
½	tsp. salt
2¼	cups (12 oz.) diced low-fat, reduced-sodium cooked ham
1	tsp. dried Italian seasoning, crushed
2	10-oz. pkgs. frozen chopped spinach, thawed and well drained
1½	cups cottage cheese
1½	cups (6 oz.) shredded mozzarella cheese

1 Preheat oven to 375°F. Cook lasagna noodles according to package directions. Drain noodles; rinse with cold water. Drain well.

2 Meanwhile, for sauce, in a medium saucepan combine the milk, onion, cornstarch, and salt. Cook and stir until thickened and bubbly. Cook and stir 2 minutes more. Spread 2 tablespoons of the sauce evenly on the bottom of a 3-quart rectangular baking dish. Stir ham and Italian seasoning into remaining sauce.

3 Arrange half of the lasagna noodles in the dish. Spread with one-third of the remaining sauce. Top with the spinach. Layer another one-third of the sauce, the cottage cheese, and half of the mozzarella cheese over the spinach. Place remaining noodles on top. Top with remaining sauce and remaining mozzarella cheese.

4 Bake, uncovered, for 30 to 35 minutes or until heated through. Let stand 10 minutes before serving (if toting, see note).

Makes 10 servings

Per serving: 237 cal., 7 g total fat (4 g sat. fat), 34 mg chol., 772 mg sodium, 23 g carbo., 2 g fiber, 20 g pro.

To tote: *Do not let stand after baking. Cover tightly. Transport in an insulated carrier.*

Denver Potato Casserole

The buttery flavor and tender texture of Yukon gold potatoes make this tater casserole a treat for brunch or supper.

Prep: 20 minutes   **Bake:** 65 minutes   **Oven:** 350°F

- 8 medium (2⅔ lb. total) Yukon gold potatoes, thinly sliced
- 1 lb. cubed cooked ham
- 1½ cups chopped green sweet pepper
- ⅔ cup chopped sweet onion
- 2 cups (8 oz.) shredded Colby-Monterey Jack cheese

1 Preheat oven to 350°F. Grease two 2-quart square baking dishes. Layer one-fourth of the potatoes, one-fourth of the ham, one-fourth of the sweet pepper, one-fourth of the onion, and one-fourth of the cheese in each baking dish. Repeat layers with the remaining ham, sweet pepper, and onion. Top with the remaining potatoes. Cover baking dishes with foil.

2 Bake for 45 minutes. Uncover and bake about 15 minutes more or until potatoes are tender. Sprinkle with remaining cheese. Bake, uncovered, about 5 minutes more or until cheese is melted.

Makes 8 servings

Per serving: 315 cal., 12 g total fat (6 g sat. fat), 56 mg chol., 1,010 mg sodium, 27 g carbo., 3 g fiber, 24 g pro.

Ham and Cheese Macaroni

Macaroni and cheese with a twist—ham and broccoli. A little red sweet pepper also adds flavor interest.

Prep: 30 minutes   **Bake:** 45 minutes   **Oven:** 350°F

- 1½ cups dried elbow macaroni
- 3 cups broccoli florets
- 1½ cups coarsely chopped red sweet pepper
- 1½ cups (8 oz.) cubed cooked ham
- 1½ cups milk
- 4½ tsp. cornstarch
- ¼ tsp. black pepper
- 1½ cups (6 oz.) cubed American cheese
- 1 cup soft bread crumbs
- 1 Tbsp. butter or margarine, melted

1 Preheat oven to 350°F. Cook macaroni according to package directions, adding broccoli and sweet pepper the last 2 minutes of cooking; drain. In a 3-quart casserole combine macaroni mixture and ham; set aside.

2 For sauce, in a small saucepan stir together milk, cornstarch, and black pepper. Cook and stir until thickened and bubbly. Add cheese; stir until melted. Stir sauce into macaroni mixture in casserole. Combine bread crumbs and butter; sprinkle over casserole.

3 Bake, uncovered, about 45 minutes or until bubbly and bread crumbs are lightly browned.

Makes 6 servings

Per serving: 373 cal., 16 g total fat (9 g sat. fat), 58 mg chol., 1,036 mg sodium, 35 g carbo., 3 g fiber, 22 g pro.

To tote: *Cover tightly. Transport in an insulated carrier.*

Ham Balls in Barbecue Sauce

Decisions, decisions. Should you serve these glistening gems with buttered spaetzle over fluffy cooked rice or eat them from toothpicks before they even make it to the table?

Prep: 25 minutes **Bake:** 45 minutes **Oven:** 350°F

4	eggs, beaten
3	cups soft bread crumbs
1	cup finely chopped onion
¼	cup milk
4	tsp. dry mustard
½	tsp. black pepper
1½	lb. ground cooked ham
1½	lb. ground pork or ground beef
1½	cups packed brown sugar
1	cup ketchup
¼	cup vinegar

1 Preheat oven to 350°F. Lightly grease two 2-quart rectangular baking dishes; set aside. In a large bowl combine eggs, bread crumbs, onion, milk, half of the mustard, and the pepper. Add ground ham and ground pork; mix well. Shape into balls, using about ⅓ cup mixture for each. Place ham balls in the prepared baking dishes.

2 In a bowl combine brown sugar, ketchup, vinegar, and the remaining mustard. Stir until sugar is dissolved. Pour over meatballs.

3 Bake, uncovered, about 45 minutes or until the internal temperature of each meatball registers 160°F.

Makes 12 servings

Per serving: 427 cal., 19 g total fat (7 g sat. fat), 143 mg chol., 1,107 mg sodium, 42 g carbo., 1 g fiber, 23 g pro.

Ham and Cheese Lasagna

Layers of smoky ham and earthy mushrooms blend with red wine to give this lasagna unique, complex flavor.

Prep: 1 hour **Bake:** 50 minutes **Stand:** 20 minutes **Oven:** 350°F

2   Tbsp. olive oil

2   cups thinly sliced celery

2   cups chopped carrots

1   cup chopped onion

2   cloves garlic, minced

3   cups sliced cremini mushrooms or other small brown mushrooms

2   cups cubed cooked ham

2   cups whipping cream

1   14.5-oz. can diced tomatoes with basil and garlic, undrained

½   cup water

¼   cup dry red wine

    Salt

    Black pepper

1½ cups (6 oz.) shredded Swiss cheese

1   cup grated Parmesan cheese

12 no-boil lasagna noodles

1 Preheat oven to 350°F. For sauce, in an extra-large skillet heat oil over medium heat. Add celery, carrots, onion, and garlic; cook and stir in hot oil for 10 minutes or just until vegetables are tender. Add mushrooms and ham. Cook, uncovered, for 10 minutes, stirring occasionally. Stir in cream, undrained tomatoes, the water, and wine. Bring to boiling; reduce heat. Simmer, uncovered, for 5 minutes. Season to taste with salt and pepper.

2 In a bowl combine Swiss cheese and Parmesan cheese. Spoon one-fourth of the sauce in a 3-quart rectangular baking dish. Sprinkle with one-fourth of the cheese mixture. Top with one-third of the lasagna noodles, overlapping as needed. Repeat layers twice. Spoon on remaining sauce and sprinkle with remaining cheese mixture. Cover tightly with foil.

3 Bake about 50 minutes or until heated through and noodles are tender when pierced with a fork. Let stand, covered, for 20 minutes before serving.

Makes 12 servings

Per serving: 376 cal., 25 g total fat (14 g sat. fat), 86 mg chol., 671 mg sodium, 22 g carbo., 2 g fiber, 15 g pro.

Zucchini-Sausage Casserole

A stuffing mixture creates a bottom layer and topper for this tasty dish. It's a great way to use your summer crop of zucchini.

Prep: 25 minutes   **Bake:** 30 minutes   **Oven:** 350°F

1   lb. bulk pork sausage

4   medium zucchini

1   10.75-oz. can condensed cream of chicken soup

1   8-oz. carton sour cream

4   cups chicken-flavor stuffing mix

⅓   cup butter or margarine, melted

    Nonstick cooking spray

1 Preheat oven to 350°F. In an extra-large skillet cook sausage until brown; drain off fat. Return sausage to skillet.

2 Meanwhile, quarter zucchini lengthwise; cut each quarter crosswise into ½-inch slices. Add zucchini to skillet.

3 In a small bowl combine soup and sour cream; stir into sausage-zucchini mixture. Set aside. In a large bowl combine stuffing mix and melted butter.

4 Lightly coat a 3-quart rectangular baking dish with cooking spray. Spoon half of the stuffing mixture into the prepared dish. Spread sausage-zucchini mixture over stuffing. Spoon remaining stuffing evenly over the top. Bake, covered, about 30 minutes or until heated through.

Makes 8 to 10 servings

Per serving: 487 cal., 34 g total fat (16 g sat. fat), 70 mg chol., 1,128 mg sodium, 28 g carbo., 2 g fiber, 14 g pro.

To tote: *Cover tightly. Transport in an insulated carrier.*

Italian-Style Spaghetti Squash

Let kids help with scooping the amazing golden strands from the baked squash halves. It's a fascinating food!

Prep: 35 minutes   **Cook:** 26 minutes   **Bake:** 35 minutes   **Stand:** 10 minutes   **Oven:** 350°F

2   medium (2¼ lb. each) spaghetti squash

½   cup water

1½ lb. bulk Italian sausage

3   cups sliced fresh mushrooms

1½ cups chopped green or red sweet pepper

⅔   cup finely chopped onion

6   cloves garlic, minced

Nonstick cooking spray

2   4.25-oz. cans chopped pitted ripe olives (optional)

1   tsp. dried Italian seasoning, crushed

¼   tsp. black pepper

3   cups purchased red pasta sauce

3   cups (12 oz.) shredded Monterey Jack cheese, mozzarella cheese, or Italian cheese blend

½   cup snipped fresh Italian (flat-leaf) parsley

1 Halve each squash crosswise; remove seeds. Place one squash, cut sides down, in a 2-quart rectangular baking dish. Add ¼ cup of the water. Cover with vented plastic wrap. Microwave on high (100 percent power) for 13 to 15 minutes or until squash is tender when pierced with fork, rearranging once for even cooking. Set aside. Repeat with the remaining squash and water in another 2-quart rectangular baking dish.

2 In an extra-large skillet cook sausage, mushrooms, sweet pepper, onion, and garlic over medium heat until sausage is cooked through, stirring to break up sausage. Drain off fat.

3 Preheat oven to 350°F. Scrape pulp from each squash (you should have about 6 cups total). Wipe out baking dishes; coat with cooking spray. Spread one-fourth of the squash in each dish. Add one-fourth of the sausage mixture and one-fourth of the olives to each dish. Sprinkle with Italian seasoning and black pepper. Top each dish with one-fourth of the pasta sauce and one-fourth of the cheese. Repeat layers with the remaining squash, sausage, olives, and pasta sauce.

4 Bake, uncovered, for 30 minutes. Sprinkle with remaining cheese. Bake about 5 minutes or until cheese is melted. Let stand for 10 minutes. Sprinkle with parsley.

Makes 12 servings

Per serving: 351 cal., 24 g total fat (11 g sat. fat), 64 mg chol., 941 mg sodium, 13 g carbo., 4 g fiber, 18 g pro.

Best-Ever Chili with Beans

This chili travels well in a slow cooker or deep casserole dish. Italian sausage and beef cubes provide heartiness. Bacon adds an interesting flavor note.

Prep: 45 minutes   **Cook:** 1¼ hours

1	lb. uncooked Italian sausage links (remove casings, if present)
3	lb. boneless beef chuck roast, cut into ½-inch cubes
1½	cups chopped green sweet pepper
5	cups water
2	15-oz. cans pinto or kidney beans, rinsed and drained
2	14.5-oz. cans diced tomatoes with onion and garlic, undrained
2	6-oz. cans tomato paste or Italian-style tomato paste
2	Tbsp. chili powder
2	or 3 fresh jalapeño chile peppers, seeded and finely chopped (see note, page 15)
½	tsp. salt
12	slices bacon, crisp-cooked, drained, and crumbled

1 In a 6-quart Dutch oven cook sausage until brown. Remove with a slotted spoon, reserving drippings in Dutch oven. Cook half of the beef cubes in the hot drippings until meat is brown; remove meat from pan. Add remaining beef cubes and sweet pepper. Cook until meat is brown; drain off fat. Return all meat to Dutch oven.

2 Stir in the water, beans, tomatoes, tomato paste, chili powder, jalapeño peppers, and salt. Bring to boiling; reduce heat. Simmer, covered, about 1¼ hours or until meat is tender. Stir in bacon; heat through.

Makes 12 servings

Per serving: 510 cal., 30 g total fat (11 g sat. fat), 104 mg chol., 1,064 mg sodium, 24 g carbo., 6 g fiber, 36 g pro.

Slow cooker directions: *Brown sausage and beef cubes as directed. Combine all ingredients, except bacon, in a 3½-, 4-, or 5-quart slow cooker. Cover and cook on low-heat setting for 8 to 10 hours or on high-heat setting for 4 to 5 hours. Stir in bacon before serving; heat through.*

To tote: *Transfer to a serving dish. Cover tightly. Transport in an insulated carrier. (Or, if desired, transport slow cooker in an insulated carrier.)*

Italian Polenta Casserole

Polenta—northern Italy's quintessential comfort food—is simply finely ground cornmeal cooked in water or broth. It is a wonderful flavor sponge that transports the tastes of any food it accompanies.

Prep: 45 minutes   **Bake:** 20 minutes   **Oven:** 400°F

2½ cups chicken broth

3 Tbsp. butter or margarine

2 cups milk

1½ cups quick-cooking polenta mix

1 3-oz. pkg. cream cheese, cut up

1 cup (4 oz.) shredded mozzarella or provolone cheese

½ cup (2 oz.) finely shredded or grated Parmesan cheese

12 oz. bulk sweet or hot Italian sausage

1 cup mushrooms, quartered

1 medium onion, cut into thin wedges

2 cloves garlic, minced

2 cups purchased pasta sauce

1 Preheat oven to 400°F. Lightly grease a 3-quart rectangular baking dish; set aside.

2 In a large saucepan bring broth and butter to boiling. Meanwhile, stir together the milk and polenta mix. Add polenta mixture to boiling broth. Cook and stir until bubbly; cook and stir for 3 to 5 minutes more or until very thick. Remove from heat. Stir in cream cheese, three-quarters of the mozzarella cheese, and half of the Parmesan cheese until well mixed. Spread two-thirds of the polenta mixture in the prepared baking dish; set aside.

3 In a large skillet cook sausage, mushrooms, onion, and garlic until meat is brown and onion is tender, stirring to break up meat; drain off fat. Add pasta sauce; heat through. Spoon sausage mixture over polenta in baking dish, spreading evenly. Spoon remaining polenta on top of sauce and sprinkle with the remaining mozzarella cheese and the remaining Parmesan cheese.

4 Bake, uncovered, about 20 minutes or until heated through and top is lightly golden.

Makes 8 servings

Per serving: 583 cal., 34 g total fat (18 g sat. fat), 92 mg chol., 1,933 mg sodium, 37 g carbo., 4 g fiber, 31 g pro.

Cheesy Sausage and Rice Bake

Crisp rice cereal is a surprising tasty ingredient.

Prep: 25 minutes   **Bake:** 45 minutes   **Stand:** 10 minutes   **Oven:** 325°F

- 2 lb. mild and/or hot bulk pork sausage
- ½ cup chopped onion
- 6 cups crisp rice cereal
- 1½ cups cooked white rice
- 2 cups (8 oz.) shredded cheddar cheese
- 6 eggs
- 2 10.75-oz. cans reduced-sodium condensed cream of celery soup
- ½ cup milk
- 1 Tbsp. butter or margarine, melted

1 Preheat oven to 325°F. Grease a 3-quart rectangular baking dish; set dish aside.

2 Cook sausage and onion in an extra-large skillet until sausage is brown and onion is tender; drain off fat. Set sausage mixture aside.

3 Meanwhile, in a large bowl combine 5 cups of the cereal and the cooked rice. Spread rice mixture evenly in the bottom of the prepared baking dish. Spoon sausage mixture over rice layer. Sprinkle with cheddar cheese.

4 In a medium mixing bowl beat eggs, soup, and milk with a wire whisk until combined; carefully pour over layers in baking dish. Press down lightly with the back of a spoon. Toss the remaining 1 cup cereal with the melted butter; sprinkle over the top.

5 Bake, uncovered, for 45 to 50 minutes or until bubbly and golden brown. Let stand 10 minutes before serving.

Makes 12 servings

Per serving: 490 cal., 33 g total fat (14 g sat. fat), 175 mg chol., 872 mg sodium, 24 g carbo., 0 g fiber, 19 g pro.

To tote: *Do not let casserole stand after baking. Cover tightly. Transport in an insulated carrier.*

Creamy Cabbage and Sausage

Cabbage lovers will enjoy this recipe. Sour cream and American cheese create a creamy dish, and the pork sausage adds flavor and spice.

Prep: 35 minutes   **Bake:** 20 minutes   **Oven:** 375°F

1½   pounds bulk pork sausage

¾   cup chopped onion

10   cups coarsely chopped cabbage

1½   cups dairy sour cream

1½   cups (6 oz.) shredded American cheese

¼   tsp. salt

¼   tsp. black pepper

1½   cups soft bread crumbs

2   Tbsp. butter or margarine, melted

1 Preheat oven to 375°F. In a Dutch oven cook sausage and onion over medium-high heat until sausage is brown. Drain off fat. Stir in cabbage. Cook, covered, over medium heat about 10 minutes or until cabbage is crisp-tender, stirring occasionally. Drain off any excess liquid.

2 Stir in sour cream, cheese, salt, and pepper. Transfer mixture to a 3-quart rectangular baking dish.

3 In a small bowl combine bread crumbs and melted butter or margarine; sprinkle over sausage mixture. Bake, uncovered, for 20 minutes or until bread crumbs are golden.

Makes 8 to 10 main-dish servings

Per serving: 520 cal., 42 g total fat (21 g sat. fat), 93 mg chol., 902 mg sodium, 12 g carbo., 2 g fiber, 18 g pro.

To tote: *Cover hot mixture tightly; tote in an insulated carrier.*

Mexican Rice and Black Bean Casserole

Pork sausage and spices from the Mexican-style stewed tomatoes give this casserole its punch of flavor. For more heat, use shredded Monterey Jack cheese with jalapeños instead of cheddar.

Prep: 20 minutes   **Bake:** 40 minutes   **Stand:** 5 minutes   **Oven:** 350°F

1   lb. bulk pork sausage

2   14.5-oz. cans Mexican-style stewed tomatoes, undrained

2   cups cooked white rice

1   15-oz. can black beans, rinsed and drained

1   medium green sweet pepper, coarsely chopped

½   cup (2 oz.) shredded cheddar cheese

Sour cream (optional)

1 Preheat oven to 350°F. In an extra-large skillet cook sausage until brown; drain off fat. Stir in tomatoes, cooked rice, black beans, and sweet pepper. Spoon into a 3-quart rectangular baking dish.

2 Bake, covered, for 40 to 45 minutes or until heated through. Remove from oven and sprinkle with cheese. Let stand 5 minutes before serving (if toting, see note). If desired, serve with sour cream.

Makes 8 servings

Per serving: 343 cal., 19 g total fat (8 g sat. fat), 40 mg chol., 811 mg sodium, 27 g carbo., 3 g fiber, 14 g pro.

To tote: *Do not let stand after baking. Cover tightly. Transport in an insulated carrier. If desired, transport sour cream in an insulated cooler with ice packs.*

Sausage-Rice Casserole

Tailor this recipe to your heat tolerance. If spicy food is your style, use more hot Italian sausage and less sweet. Or use all of one or the other.

Prep: 25 minutes   **Bake:** 50 minutes   **Oven:** 350°F

- 2 lb. uncooked sweet (mild) and/or hot Italian sausage links (remove casings, if present)
- 1 cup chopped onion
- 5 cups cooked white rice
- 2 4-oz. cans chopped green chile peppers, drained
- 2 4-oz. cans mushroom stems and pieces, drained
- 2 10.75-oz. cans condensed cream of chicken soup
- 2 cups milk
- 1½ cups (6 oz.) shredded cheddar cheese

1 Preheat oven to 350°F. Cook sausage and onion in an extra-large skillet until sausage is brown, stirring to break up sausage; drain off fat.

2 Meanwhile, in an extra-large bowl stir together rice, chile peppers, and mushrooms. Stir in soup, milk, and cheddar cheese. Stir in cooked sausage mixture. Divide mixture evenly between two 2-quart baking dishes. Bake, covered, about 50 minutes or until heated through.

Makes 12 servings

Per serving: 442 cal., 26 g total fat (11 g sat. fat), 73 mg chol., 1,056 mg sodium, 28 g carbo., 1 g fiber, 20 g pro.

Make-ahead directions: *Prepare as directed. Cover and chill for up to 24 hours. Bake, covered, in a 350°F oven for 65 to 70 minutes or until heated through.*

To tote: *Transport in an insulated carrier.*

German-Style Sausage and Potatoes

A crushed combo of aromatic seeds puts punch into this Alsatian-inspired casserole.

Prep: 25 minutes   **Cook:** 20 minutes   **Bake:** 30 minutes   **Oven:** 375°F

1½	lb. medium potatoes
1	Tbsp. anise seeds
1½	tsp. coriander seeds
1	tsp. caraway seeds
1	tsp. mustard seeds
⅓	cup beer
¼	cup vinegar
3	Tbsp. spicy brown mustard
1	Tbsp. cornstarch
1	Tbsp. granulated sugar
1	cup chopped onion
1	cup sliced celery
1	cup shredded cabbage
1	Tbsp. olive oil
12	oz. fully cooked Polish sausage, cut into ½-inch-thick slices
1	cup (4 ounces) shredded Swiss cheese

1 In a large saucepan cook potatoes, covered, in a small amount of boiling water for 20 to 25 minutes or until tender; drain. Cool, peel, and thinly slice. Using a mortar and pestle, coarsely crush the spice seeds. Combine seeds, beer, vinegar, mustard, cornstarch, and sugar; set aside.

2 Preheat oven to 375°F. In a large skillet cook onion, celery, and cabbage in hot oil for 5 to 8 minutes or just until crisp-tender. In an ungreased 2-quart rectangular or square baking dish layer half of the cabbage mixture, half of the sausage, half of the potatoes, and half of the cheese. Stir seed mixture; spoon half of the mixture over cheese. Repeat layers, reserving remaining cheese for later. Bake, uncovered, for 30 to 35 minutes or until heated through. Top with remaining cheese.

Makes 6 servings

Per serving: 415 cal., 25 g total fat (10 g sat. fat), 57 mg chol., 670 mg sodium, 31 g carbo., 3 g fiber, 17 g pro.

Italian Penne Bake

This homey casserole contains all the elements of a great pasta dish—marinara, mushrooms, onion, green sweet pepper, pepperoni, and lots of cheese.

Prep: 25 minutes   **Bake:** 30 minutes   **Oven:** 350°F

Nonstick cooking spray
- 3 cups dried penne
- 1 cup sliced fresh mushrooms
- 1 cup quartered, thinly sliced onion
- 2 medium green or red sweet peppers, cut into thin bite-size strips
- 6 oz. sliced pepperoni or Canadian-style bacon, cut up
- 1 Tbsp. bottled minced garlic
- 1 Tbsp. olive oil or vegetable oil
- 1 26- to 29-oz. jar (3 cups) marinara pasta sauce
- 1¼ cups (5 oz.) shredded Italian cheese blend

1 Preheat oven to 350°F. Lightly coat a 3-quart rectangular baking dish with cooking spray; set dish aside. Cook pasta according to package directions; drain well. Return pasta to saucepan. Meanwhile, in a large skillet cook mushrooms, onion, sweet peppers, pepperoni, and garlic in hot oil for 3 minutes. Add vegetable mixture and marinara sauce to pasta; toss to coat. Spread pasta mixture evenly in prepared baking dish.

2 Bake, covered, about 25 minutes or until heated through. Uncover and sprinkle with cheese. Bake, uncovered, about 5 minutes more or until cheese is melted.

Makes 8 servings

Per serving: 373 cal., 17 g total fat (6 g sat. fat), 27 mg chol., 905 mg sodium, 40 g carbo., 3 g fiber, 16 g pro.

- -

To tote: *Cover tightly. Transport in an insulated carrier.*

Lasagna Blanca

These serving-size roll-ups not only look and taste great, but they're super simple to prepare.

Prep: 1 hour   **Bake:** 35 minutes   **Stand:** 10 minutes   **Oven:** 350°F

- 12 dried lasagna noodles
- 1 lb. spicy bulk pork sausage
- ½ cup chopped green onions
- ½ cup chopped fresh mushrooms
- 1 cup cream-style cottage cheese
- ½ of an 8-oz. pkg. cream cheese, softened
- 1½ cups (6 oz.) shredded Monterey Jack cheese or cheddar cheese
- ½ tsp. garlic powder
- ¼ tsp. black pepper
- 1 Tbsp. butter or margarine
- 1 Tbsp. all-purpose flour
- ⅛ tsp. dried tarragon, crushed
- 1 cup milk

1 Preheat oven to 350°F. Grease a 3-quart rectangular baking dish; set aside. Cook lasagna noodles according to package directions; drain and rinse with cold water. Set aside.

2 Meanwhile, in a large skillet cook sausage, green onions, and mushrooms over medium heat until meat is cooked through, stirring to break up meat. Drain well; set aside.

3 For filling, in a bowl combine cottage cheese, cream cheese, one-third of the Monterey Jack cheese, the garlic powder, and half of the pepper; set aside.

4 Spread filling evenly over one side of each noodle. Sprinkle sausage mixture on top. Roll up each noodle into a spiral. Place lasagna rolls, seam sides down, in the prepared baking dish; set aside.

5 For sauce, in a saucepan melt butter. Stir in flour, tarragon, and the remaining pepper. Add milk. Cook and stir until slightly thickened and bubbly. Remove from heat. Stir in half of the remaining Monterey Jack cheese. Pour sauce over pasta rolls. Cover with foil.

6 Bake for 25 minutes. Uncover; sprinkle with the remaining Monterey Jack cheese. Bake about 10 minutes more or until heated through. Let stand for 10 minutes before serving.

Makes 12 servings

Per serving: 317 cal., 17 g total fat (9 g sat. fat), 54 mg chol., 378 mg sodium, 21 g carbo., 1 g fiber, 17 g pro.

Picadillo Sandwiches

The slight sweetness of raisins contrasted with the savory saltiness of olives creates balance in this delicious sandwich version of traditional Spanish picadillo [pee-kah-DEE-yoh].

Start to Finish: 35 minutes

- 2 lb. bulk pork sausage
- 2 cups chopped onion
- 2 14.5-oz. cans diced tomatoes, undrained
- 1 cup golden raisins
- ½ cup chopped green olives
- ¼ cup tomato paste
- 2 Tbsp. balsamic vinegar
- 1 tsp. ground cumin
- 1 tsp. dried oregano, crushed
- ¼ tsp. crushed red pepper (optional)
- 12 hoagie buns, split and toasted
- 2 cups (8 oz.) shredded Monterey Jack cheese

1 In an extra-large skillet cook sausage and onion for 10 minutes or until meat is brown and onion is tender, stirring to break up meat; drain off fat. Stir in undrained tomatoes, raisins, olives, tomato paste, vinegar, cumin, oregano, and, if desired, crushed red pepper. Bring to boiling; reduce heat. Simmer, uncovered, for 10 minutes or until sauce is thickened.

2 Spoon sausage mixture onto bun bottoms. Top with cheese and bun tops.

Makes 12 sandwiches

Per sandwich: 750 cal., 29 g total fat (11 g sat. fat), 66 mg chol., 1,399 mg sodium, 91 g carbo., 6 g fiber, 28 g pro.

White Bean and Sausage Rigatoni

Budget-friendly kielbasa—also known as Polish sausage—adds wonderful smokiness to this bake.

Prep: 25 minutes   **Bake:** 30 minutes   **Oven:** 375°F

10 cups (16 oz.) dried rigatoni

1   lb. cooked kielbasa

1   6-oz. can Italian-style tomato paste

½   cup dry red wine or reduced-sodium chicken broth

2   10-oz. pkg. frozen chopped spinach, thawed and drained well

4   14.5-oz. cans diced tomatoes with basil and garlic, undrained

2   15.5-oz. cans Great Northern beans, rinsed and drained

⅔   cup (3 oz.) shredded or grated Parmesan cheese

1 Preheat oven to 375°F. Cook pasta according to package directions; drain. Return to saucepan. Cut kielbasa in half lengthwise and then into bias slices. In a bowl combine tomato paste and wine.

2 Add kielbasa, tomato paste mixture, spinach, undrained tomatoes, and beans to the cooked pasta; mix well. Divide mixture between two 3-quart rectangular baking dishes. Cover with foil.

3 Bake about 25 minutes or until heated through. Sprinkle with cheese. Bake, uncovered, about 5 minutes more or until cheese is melted.

Makes 12 servings

Per serving: 564 cal., 20 g total fat (11 g sat. fat), 48 mg chol., 1,706 mg sodium, 62 g carbo., 7 g fiber, 30 g pro.

Lobster Lasagna, page 192

Chapter 4

Select Seafood Entrées

Fruited Tuna Salad

Vanilla yogurt and oranges partner in luscious dressing for this colorful tuna salad, taking everyday tuna salad up a notch or two.

Prep: 35 minutes   **Chill:** Up to 4 hours

- 2 cups vanilla yogurt
- 2 tsp. finely shredded orange peel
- 4 oranges, peeled and sectioned*
- 3 cups cubed cantaloupe and/or honeydew melon
- 3 cups halved strawberries
- ¼ cup sliced green onions
- 3 9-oz. cans solid white tuna, drained and coarsely flaked

  Leaf lettuce (optional)
- ½ cup chopped pecans, toasted

1 In a large bowl stir together vanilla yogurt and orange peel. Add orange sections, cantaloupe, strawberries, and green onions. Toss gently to coat. Add tuna; toss gently. Cover and chill for up to 4 hours.

2 To serve, if desired, place a lettuce leaf on each salad plate. Spoon tuna mixture onto plates; sprinkle salads with pecans.

Makes 8 servings

Per serving: 272 cal., 9 g total fat (2 g sat. fat), 43 mg chol., 405 mg sodium, 22 g carbo., 3 g fiber, 27 g pro.

To tote: *Transport salad and nuts in an insulated cooler with ice packs. Just before serving, sprinkle with nuts.*

---

*To save time: *Omit the fresh orange sections and substitute two 11-ounce cans mandarin orange sections, drained, for the 4 oranges. Buy a mixture of already cubed melon or melon balls from the deli or salad bar of your supermarket.*

Citrus Tuna Pasta Salad

Yellow sweet peppers, artichoke hearts, ripe olives, and a light lemon-herb dressing highlight this delicious and pretty pasta salad.

Prep: 30 minutes   **Chill:** 4 to 24 hours

- 12   oz. dried mafalda
- 2   9-oz. pkgs. frozen artichoke hearts, thawed
- 2   9.25-oz. cans chunk white tuna (water packed), drained and broken into chunks
- 2   cups sliced fresh mushrooms
- 2   cups chopped yellow sweet peppers
- ½   cup sliced, pitted ripe olives
- 1   recipe Lemon Dressing
- 2   cups cherry tomatoes, halved
- ¼   cup finely shredded Parmesan cheese

1 Cook pasta in a Dutch oven according to package directions, adding the artichoke hearts the last 5 minutes of cooking; drain. Rinse with cold water; drain again. Halve any large artichoke hearts.

2 Transfer pasta and artichoke hearts to a very large bowl. Gently stir in tuna, mushrooms, sweet peppers, and olives.

3 Pour Lemon Dressing over pasta mixture; toss to coat. Cover and chill for 4 to 24 hours. Before serving, gently stir in tomatoes and sprinkle with Parmesan cheese.

Makes 8 servings

Lemon Dressing: In a small bowl whisk together 2 teaspoons finely shredded lemon peel; ⅓ cup lemon juice; ⅓ cup rice vinegar or white wine vinegar; ¼ cup salad oil; 2 tablespoons snipped fresh thyme or basil or 2 teaspoons dried thyme or basil, crushed; 1 teaspoon sugar; ½ teaspoon black pepper; and 4 cloves garlic, minced. Makes about ¾ cup.

Per serving: 394 cal., 12 g total fat (2 g sat. fat), 31 mg chol., 407 mg sodium, 45 g carbo., 6 g fiber, 25 g pro.

To tote: *Transport salad, tomatoes, and Parmesan cheese in an insulated cooler with ice packs.*

Chilly Bow Ties and Tuna

Juicy mandarin oranges and crunchy pea pods take this tuna-pasta salad from mundane to marvelous—and make it ideal to carry for lunch.

Prep: 15 minutes   **Chill:** 4 to 24 hours

- 1 lb. dried farfalle pasta (bow ties)
- ⅔ cup light mayonnaise or salad dressing
- ⅔ cup bottled reduced-calorie Italian salad dressing
- ½ cup thinly sliced green onions (optional)
- ¼ cup orange juice
- ½ tsp. salt
- ½ tsp. black pepper
- 2 11-oz. cans mandarin orange sections, drained
- 2 12- to 12.25-oz. cans chunk white tuna (waterpack), drained and broken into chunks
- 2 cups fresh pea pods, trimmed and halved lengthwise

  Milk (optional)

1 Cook pasta according to package directions. Drain. Rinse with cold water; drain again. Transfer to a bowl.

2 Meanwhile, for dressing, in a bowl combine mayonnaise, Italian dressing, green onions (if desired), orange juice, salt, and pepper.

3 Add dressing to pasta; toss lightly to combine. Gently fold in orange sections, tuna, and pea pods. Cover and chill in the refrigerator for 4 to 24 hours. Before serving, if necessary, stir in a little milk to moisten.

Makes 12 servings

Per serving: 254 cal., 3 g total fat (1 g sat. fat), 13 mg chol., 433 mg sodium, 43 g carbo., 2 g fiber, 13 g pro.

Tuna-Noodle Casserole

This is not your ordinary tuna-noodle casserole. Mushrooms, green beans, and Swiss cheese add to its intrigue. You most likely won't have leftovers to take home!

Prep: 30 minutes   **Bake:** 30 minutes   **Oven:** 350°F

8	oz. dried medium noodles
1	16-oz. pkg. frozen whole or cut green beans
½	cup fine dry bread crumbs
2	Tbsp. butter or margarine, melted
2	Tbsp. butter or margarine
2	cups sliced fresh mushrooms
1½	cups chopped red or green sweet pepper
1	cup chopped onion
1	cup sliced celery
2	cloves garlic, minced
2	10.75-oz. cans condensed cream of mushroom or celery soup
1	cup milk
1	cup (4 oz.) shredded process Swiss or American cheese
2	9.25-oz. cans tuna (water packed), drained and flaked

1 Preheat oven to 350°F. Cook noodles according to package directions, adding the green beans the last 3 minutes of cooking. Drain and set aside. Meanwhile, toss the bread crumbs with the 2 tablespoons melted butter; set aside.

2 In an extra-large skillet melt 2 tablespoons butter over medium heat. Add mushrooms, sweet pepper, onion, celery, and garlic. Cook and stir until vegetables are tender. Add soup, milk, and cheese, stirring until cheese is melted. Stir in tuna, cooked noodles, and green beans.

3 Spoon tuna mixture into a 3-quart casserole. Sprinkle bread crumb mixture around outside edge of casserole. Bake, uncovered, for 30 to 35 minutes or until heated through and bread crumbs are golden.

Makes 12 servings

Per serving: 306 cal., 13 g total fat (6 g sat. fat), 57 mg chol., 746 mg sodium, 28 g carbo., 3 g fiber, 19 g pro.

To tote: *Cover tightly. Transport in an insulated carrier.*

Tuna with Cheese Biscuits

Tuna—the reliable pantry pal—becomes a taste treat when topped with mounds of savory cheese biscuit batter.

Prep: 15 minutes   **Bake:** 30 minutes   **Oven:** 425°F

- 1   cup chopped onion
- 1   cup chopped green sweet pepper
- ⅓   cup butter
- 2   10.75-oz. cans condensed cream of chicken soup
- 2   cups milk
- 2   9- to 9.25-oz. cans tuna, drained and flaked
- 4   tsp. lemon juice
- 2   7.75-oz. packets cheese-garlic or three-cheese complete biscuit mix

    Snipped green onions or chives

1 Preheat oven to 425°F. In a saucepan cook onion and sweet pepper in hot butter over medium heat until tender. Gently stir in soup and milk. Cook and stir until bubbly. Stir in tuna and lemon juice.

2 Transfer mixture to an ungreased 3-quart rectangular baking dish. Bake, uncovered, for 15 minutes.

3 Meanwhile, prepare biscuit mix according to package directions. Drop batter into 20 to 22 mounds on top of hot tuna mixture. Bake, uncovered, for 15 to 20 minutes more or until biscuits are golden and a wooden toothpick inserted in centers of biscuits comes out clean. If desired, garnish with green onions.

Makes 8 servings

Per serving: 564 cal., 31 g total fat (12 g sat. fat), 46 mg chol., 1,470 mg sodium, 45 g carbo., 1 g fiber, 26 g pro.

Fish Chowder

When you're hosting the potluck, bring out this chowder and you will be all the rage. It will warm you up on a chilly evening.

Prep: 35 minutes   **Cook:** 4 hours (high)

- 3 lb. fresh or frozen fish fillets (such as cod, haddock, or orange roughy)
- 2 lb. potatoes, peeled and chopped
- 3 cups chopped onions
- ¾ cup chopped celery
- ⅓ cup butter or margarine, cut up
- 3 bay leaves
- 3 tsp. salt
- ¾ tsp. dried dill
- ¾ tsp. black pepper
- 3 cups water
- ¾ cup dry vermouth, dry white wine, or water
- 3 cups whipping cream or evaporated milk
- ⅓ cup snipped fresh parsley

1 Thaw fish, if frozen. Rinse fish; pat dry. Cut fish into 2-inch pieces; cover and chill. In a 5- or 6-quart slow cooker combine potatoes, onions, celery, butter, bay leaves, salt, dill, and pepper. Stir in water and vermouth.

2 Cover and cook on high-heat setting for 3½ hours. Place fish on top of vegetable mixture. Cover and cook on high-heat setting for 30 to 45 minutes more or until fish flakes easily. Remove bay leaves. Break fish into bite-size pieces with a fork. Stir in whipping cream and parsley.

Makes 12 servings

Per serving: 450 cal., 29 g total fat (18 g sat. fat), 151 mg chol., 764 mg sodium, 19 g carbo., 2 g fiber, 25 g pro.

To tote: *Transport slow cooker in an insulated carrier.*

Smoky Salmon Casserole

Because of their high fat content, pine nuts do not keep well at room temperature. Store them in an airtight container in the refrigerator up to 3 months or freeze the nuts up to 9 months.

Prep: 30 minutes   **Bake:** 30 minutes   **Stand:** 10 minutes   **Oven:** 350°F

- 16 oz. dried bow tie pasta or penne pasta
- 2   cups chopped red sweet peppers
- 1   cup chopped green onions
- ¼   cup butter
- ¼   cup all-purpose flour
- ½   tsp. black pepper
- 5   cups milk
- 3   cups (12 oz.) shredded smoked Gouda cheese
- 1   tsp. finely shredded lemon peel
- 2   Tbsp. lemon juice
- 2   14-oz. cans quartered artichoke hearts, drained
- 2   4-oz. pieces smoked salmon, flaked and skin and bones removed
- 2   cups soft bread crumbs or panko (Japanese-style bread crumbs)
- ½   cup pine nuts
     Freshly ground black pepper

1 Preheat oven to 350°F. Cook pasta according to package directions; drain. Set aside.

2 Meanwhile, in a large skillet cook sweet peppers and green onions in hot butter over medium heat about 3 minutes or until tender. Stir in flour and the ½ teaspoon pepper. Gradually stir in milk. Cook and stir until slightly thickened and bubbly. Gradually add cheese, stirring until melted. Stir in lemon peel and lemon juice (mixture may appear curdled).

3 In a large bowl combine cooked pasta, cheese mixture, artichoke hearts, and smoked salmon. Transfer mixture to an ungreased 3-quart baking dish.

4 Sprinkle casserole with bread crumbs, pine nuts, and freshly ground pepper. Bake, uncovered, for 30 to 35 minutes or until mixture is heated through and crumbs are golden. Let stand for 10 minutes before serving.

Makes 12 servings

Per serving: 470 cal., 19 g total fat (10 g sat. fat), 74 mg chol., 780 mg sodium, 45 g carbo., 4 g fiber, 30 g pro.

Salmon with Feta and Pasta

The juice in most tomatoes can dilute the flavors of the other ingredients. Because dense and meaty roma tomatoes contain less juice, they are the best choice for this colorful recipe.

Start to Finish: 25 minutes

- 1½ lb. fresh or frozen skinless salmon fillet
- Salt
- 1 lb. dried rotini pasta
- Nonstick cooking spray
- 4 cloves garlic, minced
- 4 cups chopped roma tomatoes
- 2 cups sliced green onions
- ⅔ cup sliced pitted ripe olives
- ⅓ cup snipped fresh basil
- 1 tsp. coarsely ground black pepper
- 4 tsp. olive oil
- 2 4-oz. pkg. crumbled feta cheese
- Fresh basil sprigs (optional)

1 Thaw fish, if frozen. Rinse fish; pat dry with paper towels. Cut fish into 1-inch pieces; lightly season with salt. Set aside.

2 Cook pasta according to pasta directions. Drain. Return pasta to hot pan; cover and keep warm.

3 Meanwhile, lightly coat a nonstick skillet with cooking spray; heat skillet over medium-high heat. Add garlic. Cook and stir for 15 seconds. Add fish to skillet. Cook fish for 4 to 6 minutes or until fish begins to flake easily when tested with a fork, turning fish pieces occasionally. Stir in tomatoes, green onions, olives, basil, and pepper. Heat through.

4 In a bowl toss together warm pasta, olive oil, salmon mixture, and cheese. If desired, garnish with basil sprigs.

Makes 10 servings

Per serving: 373 cal., 13 g total fat (5 g sat. fat), 56 mg chol., 443 mg sodium, 41 g carbo., 3 g fiber, 24 g pro.

Trout Amandine

Coarse, crisp panko crumbs and buttery almonds provide the super crunchy crust on these fish fillets.

Prep: 15 minutes   **Bake:** 4 to 6 minutes per ½-inch thickness   **Oven:** 450°F

- 8   4-oz. fresh or frozen skinless cod, tilapia, trout, or halibut fillets, ½ to 1 inch thick
- ½   cup buttermilk or milk
- 1   cup panko (Japanese-style bread crumbs) or fine dry bread crumbs
- ¼   cup snipped fresh parsley
- 1   tsp. dry mustard
- ½   tsp. salt
- ¼   tsp. black pepper
- ½   cup sliced almonds, coarsely chopped
- 2   Tbsp. butter, melted

1 Thaw fish, if frozen. Preheat oven to 450°F. Grease a shallow baking pan; set aside. Rinse fish; pat dry with paper towels. Measure thickness of fish.

2 In a shallow dish pour in buttermilk . In another shallow dish combine bread crumbs, parsley, dry mustard, salt, and pepper. Dip fish into buttermilk, then coat both sides of fish with crumb mixture.

Place coated fish in prepared baking pan. Sprinkle fish with almonds. Drizzle melted butter over fish.

3 Bake, uncovered, for 4 to 6 minutes per ½-inch thickness of fish or until fish begins to flake easily when tested with a fork.

Makes 8 servings

Per serving: 200 cal., 8 g total fat (2 g sat. fat), 56 mg chol., 266 mg sodium, 8 g carbo., 1 g fiber, 24 g pro.

Cheesy Shrimp and Rice

Swiss and cheddar cheeses combine with mushroom soup for this shrimp dish. Purchase deveined shrimp to keep prep time down.

Prep: 40 minutes   **Bake:** 35 minutes   **Stand:** 10 minutes   **Oven:** 375°F

- 2   6.2-oz. pkgs. quick-cooking long grain and wild rice mix
- 2   cups chopped red sweet peppers
- 2   cups chopped celery
- 2   cups chopped onions
- ⅓   cup butter or margarine
- 2   10.75-oz. cans condensed golden mushroom soup
- 2   cups (8 oz.) shredded Swiss cheese
- 2   cups (8 oz.) shredded cheddar cheese
- ½   tsp. black pepper
- 2   pounds cooked, peeled, and deveined medium shrimp (remove tails, if present)
  - Lemon slices (optional)

1 Preheat oven to 375°F. Prepare rice mixes according to package directions. Meanwhile, in a 4-quart Dutch oven cook and stir sweet peppers, celery, and onions in hot butter about 5 minutes or just until tender.

2 In a very large bowl combine the cooked rice, cooked vegetable mixture, soup, Swiss cheese, half of the cheddar cheese, and the black pepper. Stir in the shrimp. Spoon mixture into two 3-quart rectangular baking dishes.

3 Bake, covered, about 35 minutes or until heated through, rotating baking dishes halfway through baking. Remove from oven; sprinkle with remaining cheddar cheese. Let stand 10 minutes before serving (if toting, see note). If desired, garnish with lemon slices.

Makes 12 servings

Per serving: 452 cal., 20 g total fat (11 g sat. fat), 205 mg chol., 1,274 mg sodium, 32 g carbo., 2 g fiber, 35 g pro.

To tote: *Do not let stand after baking. Cover tightly. Transport in an insulated carrier.*

Baked Shrimp Curry

A trio of spices—curry powder, paprika, and nutmeg—uniquely flavors the cream sauce. The condiments chutney, orange peel, coconut, and peanuts supply additional flavor interest.

Prep: 30 minutes   **Bake:** 15 minutes   **Oven:** 400°F

- 2   lb. fresh or frozen peeled, cooked shrimp
- ¼   cup butter or margarine
- 2   Tbsp. all-purpose flour
- 1   Tbsp. curry powder
- ½   tsp. paprika
- ⅛   tsp. ground nutmeg
- 2   cups half-and-half, light cream, or milk
- 2   Tbsp. dry sherry (optional)
- 2   tsp. lemon juice
- 2   tsp. grated fresh ginger
- ⅛   tsp. Worcestershire sauce
- 4   cups hot cooked rice
  Chutney, finely shredded orange peel, flaked coconut, and/or chopped peanuts (optional)

1 Thaw shrimp, if frozen. Rinse shrimp; pat dry. Preheat oven to 400°F. In a saucepan melt butter. Stir in flour, curry powder, paprika, and nutmeg. Stir in half-and-half all at once. Cook and stir over medium heat until thickened and bubbly. Cook and stir 1 minute more. Stir in shrimp, sherry (if desired), lemon juice, ginger, and Worcestershire sauce; heat through. Transfer to an ungreased 2-quart casserole.

2 Bake, uncovered, about 15 minutes or until bubbly and lightly browned. Serve with rice. If desired, pass condiments to sprinkle on each serving.

Makes 8 servings

Per serving: 358 cal., 15 g total fat (9 g sat. fat), 260 mg chol., 342 mg sodium, 27 g carbo., 1 g fiber, 28 g pro.

To tote: *Cover tightly. Transport casserole and hot cooked rice, separately, in an insulated carrier. If desired, transport condiments in an insulated cooler with ice packs.*

Crawfish Fettuccine

This is a great way to fix crawfish at home when it's in season. You also can fix the dish with shrimp.

Prep: 25 minutes   **Bake:** 20 minutes   **Oven:** 350°F

1   lb. fresh or frozen peeled, cooked crawfish tails*

1   lb. dried fettuccine, broken

1   cup coarsely chopped green sweet pepper

¾   cup chopped onion

4   cloves garlic, minced

¼   cup butter or margarine

3   Tbsp. all-purpose flour

¼   to ½ tsp. ground red pepper

¼   tsp. salt

2   cups half-and-half, light cream, or milk

1½   cups (6 oz.) shredded American cheese

2   Tbsp. snipped fresh parsley

⅓   cup grated Parmesan cheese

1 Thaw crawfish, if frozen. Preheat oven to 350°F. In a Dutch oven cook fettuccine according to package directions. Drain; return to Dutch oven.

2 Meanwhile, for sauce, in a large saucepan cook sweet pepper, onion, and garlic in hot butter about 5 minutes or until tender. Stir in flour, ground red pepper, and salt. Add half-and-half all at once. Cook and stir over medium heat until thickened and bubbly. Add cheese, stirring until melted. Remove from heat; stir in crawfish and parsley. Pour sauce over fettuccine, tossing gently to coat. Spoon mixture into an ungreased 3-quart rectangular baking dish. Sprinkle with Parmesan cheese. Bake, covered, for 20 to 25 minutes or until heated through.

Makes 8 servings

Per serving: 506 cal., 22 g total fat (13 g sat. fat), 123 mg chol., 574 mg sodium, 51 g carbo., 2 g fiber, 25 g pro.

---

*Note: *If you aren't able to find peeled crawfish tails, purchase 4 pounds of whole, head-on crawfish. This will yield 1 pound. Allow about 1 hour to peel crawfish.*

To tote: *Transport in an insulated carrier.*

Basil-Lemon Shrimp Linguine

This light and lovely linguine looks as fresh and promising as the first day of spring—and at a mere 330 calories per serving, it will help keep you in shape for summer.

Start to Finish: 30 minutes

- 2 lb. fresh or frozen large shrimp in shells
- 12 oz. dried linguine or fettuccine
- 1 lb. fresh asparagus spears, trimmed and cut diagonally into 1-inch pieces

  Nonstick cooking spray
- 4 cloves garlic, minced
- 2 cups thin red, yellow, and/or green sweet pepper strips
- 2 tsp. finely shredded lemon peel
- ½ tsp. salt
- ½ tsp. black pepper
- ½ cup snipped fresh basil
- ½ cup sliced green onions
- ¼ cup lemon juice
- 2 Tbsp. olive oil

  Fresh basil sprigs (optional)

  Lemon wedges (optional)

1 Thaw shrimp, if frozen. Peel and devein shrimp, leaving tails intact if desired. Rinse shrimp; pat dry with paper towels; set aside.

2 Cook pasta according to package directions, adding asparagus during the last 3 minutes of cooking. Drain. Return pasta mixture to hot pan; cover and keep warm.

3 Meanwhile, lightly coat a nonstick skillet with cooking spray; heat over medium heat. Add garlic. Cook and stir for 15 seconds. Add pepper strips. Cook and stir for 2 minutes or until crisp-tender. Add shrimp, lemon peel, salt, and black pepper. Cook and stir for 3 minutes or until shrimp are opaque. Remove from heat.

4 Add shrimp mixture to warm pasta mixture. Add snipped fresh basil, the green onions, lemon juice, and oil; toss gently to coat. Transfer to serving plates. If desired, garnish each serving with basil sprigs and/or lemon wedges.

Makes 8 servings

Per serving: 336 cal., 6 g total fat (1 g sat. fat), 172 mg chol., 463 mg sodium, 39 g carbo., 4 g fiber, 31 g pro.

Lobster Lasagna

Lobster, Brie cheese, and asparagus combine for this very sophisticated lasagna.

Prep: 45 minutes   **Bake:** 25 minutes   **Stand:** 5 minutes   **Oven:** 475°F/400°F

- 2 lb. fresh asparagus spears, cut into 2-inch pieces
- 2 Tbsp. olive oil
- 1 9-oz. pkg. no-boil lasagna noodles
- ¼ cup butter or margarine
- ¼ cup all-purpose flour
- 1½ cups chicken broth
- ¼ tsp. white pepper
- 2 4½-oz. rounds Brie cheese, peeled and cubed
- ¼ cup dry sherry (optional)
- 2½ cups chopped cooked lobster meat* or two 6- or 8-oz. pkgs. flake-style imitation lobster
- ⅔ cup finely shredded Parmesan cheese
- 1 cup chopped tomato

1 Preheat oven to 475°F. Grease a 3-quart rectangular baking dish; set dish aside. Place asparagus pieces in a 13×9×2-inch baking pan; toss with oil. Bake, uncovered, for 5 to 8 minutes or until crisp-tender; cool.

2 Meanwhile, separate lasagna noodles and soak in water for 15 minutes; drain. Reduce oven temperature to 400°F.

3 For sauce, in a small saucepan melt butter over medium heat; stir in flour. Cook and stir about 5 minutes or until flour mixture is lightly browned. Stir in broth and white pepper. Cook and stir until thickened and bubbly. Reduce heat to low. Stir in Brie until almost melted. If desired, stir in sherry.

4 Place one-third of the lasagna noodles in the bottom of the prepared baking dish, overlapping or trimming as necessary to fit. Top with ⅓ cup of the sauce, half of the asparagus, and half of the lobster. Sprinkle with a little of the Parmesan cheese.

5 Repeat layers with another one-third of the noodles, ⅓ cup of the sauce, remaining asparagus, and remaining lobster. Sprinkle with a little more of the Parmesan cheese. Top with remaining lasagna noodles, chopped tomato, remaining sauce, and remaining Parmesan cheese.

6 Bake, covered, for 20 minutes. Uncover and bake for 5 to 10 minutes more or until bubbly. Let stand 5 minutes before serving (if toting, see note).

Makes 12 servings

Per serving: 283 cal., 15 g total fat (8 g sat. fat), 67 mg chol., 438 mg sodium, 19 g carbo., 1 g fiber, 18 g pro.

To tote: *Do not let stand after baking. Cover tightly. Transport in an insulated carrier.*

*Note: *For 2½ cups cooked lobster meat, in a 3-quart saucepan cook four 8-ounce lobster tails in boiling water, uncovered, for 8 to 12 minutes or until shells turn bright red and meat is tender. Drain. Remove shells and coarsely chop lobster meat.*

Lobster Rolls

Lobster for a potluck? Why not? Frozen lobster takes less time to cook than many meats. Of course you'll want to reserve these sandwiches for only the most important celebrations!

Prep: 20 minutes   **Stand:** 20 minutes   **Chill:** 1 hour

4   8-oz. fresh or frozen lobster tails

⅔   cup mayonnaise or salad dressing

4   green onions, thinly sliced

2   Tbsp. finely chopped red sweet pepper

2   tsp. finely shredded lemon peel

2   tsp. lemon juice

     Several drops bottled hot pepper sauce

8   6-inch pieces baguette-style French bread, halved lengthwise, or 8 hoagie buns, split

8   romaine leaves

1 Thaw lobster tails, if frozen. In a large saucepan cook lobster tails, uncovered, in boiling water for 8 to 12 minutes or until shells turn bright red and meat is tender; drain. (Cook lobster half at a time if necessary.) Let stand about 20 minutes or until cool enough to handle. Remove and discard shells. Coarsely chop meat (you should have about 4 cups).

2 In a medium bowl combine lobster meat, mayonnaise, green onions, sweet pepper, lemon peel, lemon juice, and hot pepper sauce. Cover and chill for 1 hour.

3 Hollow out the bottom half of each baguette, leaving a thick shell. Line the bottom of each baguette with a romaine leaf; spoon lobster mixture on top of romaine. Place top half of baguette on lobster mixture.

Makes 8 servings

Per serving: 575 cal., 19 g total fat (3 g sat. fat), 62 mg chol., 1,197 mg sodium, 73 g carbo., 5 g fiber, 27 g pro.

- -

To tote: *Wrap each lobster roll in plastic wrap. Transport in an insulated cooler with ice packs. Serve within 2 hours.*

Caribbean Crab Wraps

Call upon these festive wraps whenever sandwich boredom sets in—they're guaranteed to enliven the palate.

Start to Finish: 25 minutes

2 8-oz. pkg. chunk-style imitation crabmeat, flaked

2 medium zucchini, shredded

2 cups coarsely chopped pineapple

¼ cup chopped green onions

¼ cup canned diced green chile peppers

1 tsp. salt

½ tsp. black pepper

¾ cup tub-style cream cheese spread with chive and onion

6 10-inch tomato-flavor flour tortillas

⅔ cup shredded coconut, toasted

1 In a bowl toss together crabmeat, zucchini, pineapple, green onions, chile peppers, salt, and black pepper. Set aside.

2 To assemble, spread 2 tablespoons cream cheese over one side of each tortilla. Arrange some of the crabmeat mixture over the cream cheese. Sprinkle with some coconut. Roll up each of the wraps. Serve immediately.

Makes 6 servings

Per serving: 386 cal., 18 g total fat (11 g sat. fat), 45 mg chol., 1,591 mg sodium, 49 g carbo., 15 g fiber, 17 g pro.

Crab and Spinach Pasta with Fontina

Get to know fontina. Its mild, buttery, and slightly nutty taste makes it the perfect cheese for most any use. This cheese has excellent meltability.

Prep: 20 minutes   **Bake:** 30 minutes   **Stand:** 10 minutes   **Oven:** 375°F

1   lb. dried bow tie pasta

2   10-oz. pkg. frozen chopped spinach, thawed and drained well

4   6- to 6.5-oz. cans crabmeat, drained, flaked, and cartilage removed

2   26-oz. jars pasta sauce

3   cups shredded fontina cheese

1 Preheat oven to 375°F. Cook pasta according to package directions. Drain. Return pasta to hot pan; cover and keep warm. Meanwhile, in a bowl combine spinach and crabmeat.

2 Cover bottom of a 3-quart rectangular baking dish with 2 cups of the sauce. Top with pasta. Top pasta evenly with crab mixture. Sprinkle with 1½ cups of the cheese. Top with remaining sauce. Sprinkle with remaining 1½ cups cheese.

3 Bake, uncovered, for 30 to 35 minutes or until sauce is bubbly around edges and cheese is slightly golden. Let stand for 10 minutes before serving.

Makes 12 servings

Per serving: 376 cal., 11 g total fat (6 g sat. fat), 83 mg chol., 1,061 mg sodium, 45 g carbo., 5 g fiber, 27 g pro.

Macaroni and Brie with Crab

This is definitely not your everyday mac and cheese. Prepare this luxuriously rich, definitely decadent dish only when you need to dive into indulgence.

Prep: 30 minutes   **Bake:** 20 minutes   **Oven:** 350°F

Nonstick cooking spray

1 medium sweet onion, halved and thinly sliced

¼ cup butter

1 lb. dried medium shell pasta

⅓ cup all-purpose flour

¾ tsp. salt

½ tsp. black pepper

3 cups milk

1 lb. Brie cheese, trimmed and chopped (if desired, reserve small wedges for garnish)

2 6- to 6.5-oz. cans crabmeat, drained, flaked, and cartilage removed

3 slices firm white bread, torn into large pieces

8 small Brie cheese wedges for topping (optional)

1 Preheat oven to 350°F. Lightly coat eight 14- to 16-ounce individual baking dishes with cooking spray; set aside. In a skillet cook onion in hot butter over medium-low heat for 15 to 20 minutes or until very tender and golden brown, stirring occasionally.

2 Meanwhile, cook pasta according to package directions. Drain. Return pasta to hot pan; cover and keep warm.

3 For sauce, add flour, salt, and pepper to onion in skillet; cook and stir about 1 minute or until combined. Add milk all at once. Cook and stir until slightly thickened and bubbly. Gradually add the chopped cheese; cook and stir over medium-low heat until cheese melts. Stir into warm pasta; toss lightly to combine. Gently fold in crab. Transfer crab mixture to baking dishes.

4 Place bread pieces in food processor; cover and process to coarse crumbs. Sprinkle crumbs over pasta mixture.

5 Bake, uncovered, for 20 to 25 minutes or until heated through and crumbs are golden brown. If desired, add a small wedge of Brie to each dish the last 5 minutes of baking time.

Makes 8 servings

Per serving: 595 cal., 27 g total fat (16 g sat. fat), 137 mg chol., 905 mg sodium, 57 g carbo., 2 g fiber, 31 g pro.

Seafood Rice Casserole

This hearty casserole features shrimp, budget-conscious imitation crabmeat, rice, and vegetables. It's perfect party food.

Prep: 30 minutes   **Bake:** 30 minutes   **Oven:** 350°F

- 1   12-oz. pkg. frozen peeled, cooked shrimp
- 3   cups sliced fresh mushrooms
- 1   small onion, cut into thin wedges
- ½   cup chopped green sweet pepper
- 1   Tbsp. vegetable oil
- 2½   cups cooked white rice
- 1   8-oz. can sliced water chestnuts, drained
- 1   cup mayonnaise or salad dressing
- 1   cup tomato juice
- ¼   tsp. salt
- ⅛   tsp. black pepper
- 1   6- or 8-oz. pkg. flake-style imitation crabmeat
- ½   cup sliced almonds, toasted

1 Thaw shrimp, if frozen. Rinse shrimp; pat dry. Preheat oven to 350°F. In a large skillet cook mushrooms, onion, and sweet pepper in hot oil over medium heat about 5 minutes or until tender. In a very large bowl stir together cooked vegetables, cooked rice, water chestnuts, mayonnaise, tomato juice, salt, and pepper; mix well. Stir in shrimp and imitation crabmeat.

2 Spoon seafood mixture into an ungreased 2-quart rectangular baking dish. Bake, covered, for 30 to 35 minutes or until bubbly. Just before serving, sprinkle with almonds.

Makes 8 servings

Per serving: 419 cal., 30 g total fat (4 g sat. fat), 103 mg chol., 618 mg sodium, 24 g carbo., 2 g fiber, 17 g pro.

To tote: *Cover tightly. Transport casserole and almonds in an insulated carrier.*

Farm-Style Green Beans, page 225

Chapter 5

Essential
Sides

Marinated Vegetable Salad

This vegetable salad can be refrigerated for up to 24 hours, making it a blessing when you don't have time to make the salad the day of your picnic, party, or potluck.

Prep: 20 minutes   **Stand:** 30 minutes

4   medium tomatoes or 8 roma tomatoes, cut into wedges

2   medium green sweet peppers, cut into small squares

2½ cups thinly sliced zucchini or yellow summer squash (2 medium)

½   cup thinly sliced red onion

¼   cup snipped fresh parsley

¼   cup olive oil

¼   cup balsamic or wine vinegar

¼   cup water

2   Tbsp. snipped fresh thyme or basil or 1 tsp. dried thyme or basil, crushed

2   cloves garlic, minced

1 In a bowl combine tomatoes, sweet peppers, zucchini, onion, and parsley; set aside.

2 For dressing, in a screw-top jar combine oil, vinegar, water, thyme, and garlic. Cover and shake well. Pour dressing over vegetable mixture. Toss lightly to coat.

3 Let vegetable mixture stand at room temperature for 30 to 60 minutes, stirring occasionally. (Or cover and chill for 4 to 24 hours, stirring once or twice. Let stand at room temperature about 30 minutes before serving.) Serve with a slotted spoon.

Makes 12 servings

Per serving: 64 cal., 5 g total fat (1 g sat. fat), 0 mg chol., 6 mg sodium, 5 g carbo., 1 g fiber, 1 g pro.

To tote: *Cover room-temperature salad tightly. Transport in an insulated carrier. Transport chilled salad in an insulated cooler with ice packs.*

Apple-Rice Salad

Hearty grains of brown and wild rices complement crisp apples, crunchy celery, and sunflower seeds for a healthful autumn salad. Add leftover turkey or chicken cubes to make it a main dish.

Prep: 50 minutes   **Chill:** 2 hours

- 1½   cups water
- ⅔   cup uncooked brown rice
- ⅔   cup uncooked wild rice, rinsed and drained
- 4   cups chopped apples
- 2   cups thinly sliced celery
- ½   cup shelled sunflower seeds
- ½   cup dried currants or dried cranberries
- ¼   cup balsamic vinegar
- 2   Tbsp. olive oil
- 4   tsp. honey
- 4   tsp. brown or Dijon-style mustard
- 4   tsp. finely shredded orange peel
- 2   cloves garlic, minced
- ½   tsp. salt
- Lettuce leaves (optional)

1 In a saucepan bring the water to boiling. Add brown rice and wild rice. Return to boiling; reduce heat. Simmer, covered, for 40 to 45 minutes or until rice is tender. Drain. Transfer to a bowl; cover and chill in the refrigerator for 2 hours.

2 Add apples, celery, sunflower seeds, and currants to the chilled rice mixture; stir to mix together.

3 For dressing, in a screw-top jar combine the vinegar, oil, honey, mustard, orange peel, garlic, and salt. Cover and shake well. Drizzle over rice mixture; toss lightly to coat. Serve immediately on lettuce leaves. Or cover and chill in the refrigerator up to 4 hours.

Makes 12 servings

Per serving: 191 cal., 6 g total fat (1 g sat. fat), 0 mg chol., 143 mg sodium, 32 g carbo., 4 g fiber, 4 g pro.

Cranberry-Broccoli Salad

This salad is a good holiday dish. Because cranberries freeze so well, you can make it year-round. No frozen cranberries? Omit the sugar and use dried cranberries instead.

Prep: 20 minutes   **Chill:** 2 to 24 hours

- 1¼ cups cranberries, chopped
- ¼ cup sugar
- 4 cups broccoli florets
- 4 cups packaged shredded cabbage with carrot (coleslaw mix)
- ½ cup chopped walnuts
- ½ cup raisins
- ⅓ cup chopped onion
- 6 slices bacon, crisp-cooked, drained, and crumbled
- 1 cup light mayonnaise dressing or mayonnaise
- ¼ cup sugar
- 1 Tbsp. vinegar

1 In a small bowl combine the chopped cranberries and ¼ cup sugar. Cover and chill until serving time (berries will juice out).

2 In a very large bowl combine broccoli, cabbage, walnuts, raisins, onion, and bacon.

3 In another small bowl stir together the mayonnaise dressing, ¼ cup sugar, and vinegar.

Drizzle over broccoli mixture; toss gently to coat. Cover and chill for 2 to 24 hours.

4 Just before serving, gently fold cranberry mixture into salad.

Makes 10 to 12 servings

Per serving: 229 cal., 14 g total fat (3 g sat. fat), 11 mg chol., 225 mg sodium, 26 g carbo., 3 g fiber, 4 g pro.

To tote: *Transport in an insulated cooler with ice packs.*

Minted Wild Rice Salad

Beautiful and tasty, this salad is one you'll be asked for again and again. Mint provides a refreshing flavor.

Prep: 20 minutes   **Cook:** 40 minutes   **Chill:** 2 to 8 hours

1   cup uncooked wild rice, rinsed and drained

1½ cups chopped tomatoes

1   cup chopped yellow, green, or red sweet pepper

1   cup chopped green onions

⅔   cup golden raisins or dried cherries

⅔   cup chopped pecans, toasted

½   cup snipped fresh mint

⅓   cup olive oil

⅓   cup lemon juice

½   tsp. salt

½   tsp. black pepper

1 Cook wild rice according to package directions; drain and cool.

2 In a large bowl combine cooled rice, tomatoes, sweet pepper, green onions, raisins, pecans, and mint; set aside.

3 In a small bowl combine olive oil, lemon juice, salt, and black pepper; mix well. Pour over wild rice mixture, tossing to coat. Cover and chill for 2 to 8 hours.

Makes 12 servings

Per serving: 184 cal., 11 g total fat (1 g sat. fat), 0 mg chol., 105 mg sodium, 21 g carbo., 3 g fiber, 3 g pro.

To tote: *Transport in an insulated cooler with ice packs.*

Garden and Grain Salad

This basmati rice and lentil salad is dressed with a lemony Dijon Dressing. Feta cheese, although optional, complements the lemon perfectly.

Prep: 40 minutes   **Cool:** 20 minutes   **Chill:** 4 to 24 hours

- 4 cups water
- ½ tsp. salt
- 1 cup brown lentils, rinsed and drained
- 1 cup uncooked basmati rice or long grain rice
- 1½ cups coarsely chopped red, yellow, and/or green sweet pepper
- 1 cup chopped carrot
- 1 cup sliced celery
- ½ cup chopped seedless cucumber
- ½ cup chopped radishes
- ½ cup chopped green onions
- 1 recipe Dijon Dressing
- 1 cup (4 oz.) crumbled feta cheese (optional)

1. In a medium saucepan bring water and salt to boiling; stir in lentils. Return to boiling; reduce heat. Simmer, covered, about 25 minutes or until lentils are tender but not soft. Drain well. Spoon lentils into a very large bowl; set lentils aside.

2. Meanwhile, cook rice according to package directions. Add rice to lentils in bowl. Set lentils and rice aside for about 20 minutes or until cool.

3. Gently stir sweet pepper, carrot, celery, cucumber, radishes, and green onions into cooled lentil-rice mixture. Add Dijon Dressing; toss gently to coat. Cover and chill for 4 to 24 hours. If desired, sprinkle with feta cheese.

Makes 16 servings

Dijon Dressing: In a blender container combine ¾ cup olive oil, ⅓ cup lemon juice, ⅓ cup Dijon-style mustard, ½ teaspoon salt, ¼ teaspoon black pepper, and 2 cloves garlic, minced. Cover and blend until smooth. Makes about 1½ cups.

Per serving: 190 cal., 11 g total fat (1 g sat. fat), 0 mg chol., 186 mg sodium, 20 g carbo., 5 g fiber, 5 g pro.

To tote: *Transport salad and, if desired, feta cheese in an insulated cooler with ice packs.*

Lox-Style Pasta Salad

Lox is fresh salmon that has been brined, then either hot- or cold-smoked. A bit saltier than other varieties of smoked salmon, it has unsurpassed silky texture.

Prep: 40 minutes   **Chill:** 4 to 24 hours

12 oz. dried medium shell macaroni

2 hard-cooked eggs, chopped

1 4-oz. pkg. thinly sliced smoked salmon (lox-style), chopped

⅓ cup chopped red onion

2 Tbsp. capers, rinsed and drained

1 8-oz. carton sour cream

⅓ cup milk

¼ cup chopped fresh dill

2 Tbsp. mayonnaise or salad dressing

½ tsp. salt

¼ tsp. freshly ground black pepper

Milk (optional)

1 Cook pasta according to package directions; drain. Rinse with cold water; drain again. Transfer to a large bowl.

2 In same bowl add eggs, salmon, onion, and drained capers.

3 For dressing, in a bowl combine sour cream, the ⅓ cup milk, dill, mayonnaise, salt, and pepper. Drizzle over pasta mixture; toss lightly to coat. Cover and chill in the refrigerator for 4 to 24 hours. Before serving, if necessary, stir in additional milk to moisten.

Makes 10 servings

Per serving: 230 cal., 9 g total fat (4 g sat. fat), 58 mg chol., 441 mg sodium, 27 g carbo., 1 g fiber, 9 g pro.

Italian Basil, Tomato, and Pasta Salad

This recipes uses lots of basil. Make this salad when basil is in full supply in the summer.

Prep: 45 minutes   **Chill:** 4 to 24 hours

- ½   cup red wine vinegar
- 2   Tbsp. Dijon-style mustard
- ¼   tsp. black pepper
- 2   cloves garlic, minced
- ½   cup olive oil
- ½   cup slivered fresh basil
- 8   oz. dried pasta (such as rotini, bow ties, shells, cavatelli, or penne)
- 2   9-oz. pkgs. frozen cut green beans
- 6   medium tomatoes, cut into thin wedges
- 1   cup sliced pitted kalamata olives or ripe olives
- 2   cups loosely packed fresh basil leaves
- ¾   cup (3 oz.) finely shredded Parmesan cheese
- 3   Tbsp. snipped fresh parsley

1 For dressing, in a small bowl whisk together vinegar, mustard, pepper, and garlic. Gradually whisk in oil. Stir in the slivered basil. Set dressing aside.

2 Cook pasta according to package directions; drain. Rinse with cold water; drain again.

3 Meanwhile, in a large saucepan cook frozen beans according to package directions; drain. Rinse with cold water; drain again.

4 Toss one-third of the dressing with the cooked pasta; place pasta in the bottom of a very large salad bowl. Layer ingredients on top of the pasta in the following order: cooked green beans, tomatoes, and olives. Top with remaining dressing. Sprinkle with the basil leaves, the Parmesan cheese, and parsley. Cover and chill for 4 to 24 hours. To serve, toss lightly to combine.

Makes 16 servings

Per serving: 173 cal., 10 g total fat (2 g sat. fat), 5 mg chol., 167 mg sodium, 17 g carbo., 3 g fiber, 5 g pro.

- -

To tote: *Transport in an insulated cooler with ice packs.*

Deviled Egg Salad

Take this fresh and colorful dish to your next potluck. It will be the most popular offering on the salad table.

Start to Finish: 30 minutes

- 12 hard-cooked eggs
- 6 Tbsp. mayonnaise or salad dressing
- 2 Tbsp. snipped fresh dill
- 2 cloves garlic, minced
- ⅛ tsp. bottled hot pepper sauce
- ¼ tsp. salt
- ⅔ cup olive oil
- ¼ cup tarragon vinegar
- 2 Tbsp. snipped fresh dill
- 4 tsp. Dijon-style mustard
- 2 cloves garlic, minced
- ½ tsp. salt
- ½ tsp. bottled hot pepper sauce
- 12 cups torn Boston or Bibb lettuce
- 4 cups grape or cherry tomatoes, halved, if desired
- 1½ cups chopped red sweet peppers
- 8 slices bacon, crisp-cooked, drained, and crumbled
- 6 green onions, sliced

1 Remove shells and halve hard-cooked eggs lengthwise; remove yolks. Set aside whites. Place yolks in a bowl; mash with a fork. Add mayonnaise, the 2 tablespoons snipped dill, the 2 cloves minced garlic, the ⅛ teaspoon hot pepper sauce, and the ¼ teaspoon salt. Spoon yolk mixture into egg white halves. Set aside.

2 For vinaigrette, in a screw-top jar combine olive oil, vinegar, the 2 tablespoons snipped dill, the Dijon-style mustard, the 2 cloves minced garlic, the ½ teaspoon salt, and the ½ teaspoon bottled hot pepper sauce. Cover and shake well. Set aside.

3 To serve, use two large serving platters. On each platter arrange half of the lettuce, tomatoes, sweet peppers, bacon, and green onions. Arrange half of the stuffed eggs on each lettuce mixture. Shake vinaigrette and drizzle over the salads.

Makes 12 servings

Per serving: 269 cal., 22 g total fat (4 g sat. fat), 254 mg chol., 427 mg sodium, 8 g carbo., 2 g fiber, 11 g pro.

Broccoli-Cauliflower Salad

Straightforward and delicious, this broccoli and cauliflower salad is a classic dish that is hard to resist. A little horseradish and lemon add zip to the mayonnaise dressing.

Prep: 20 minutes   **Chill:** 4 to 24 hours

4   cups small cauliflower florets

3   cups small broccoli florets

4   green onions, thinly sliced

¾   cup sliced radishes

½   cup shredded carrot

1   cup mayonnaise or salad dressing

2   Tbsp. sugar

1   Tbsp. lemon juice

2   tsp. prepared horseradish

½   tsp. salt

½   tsp. black pepper

6   slices bacon, crisp-cooked, drained, and crumbled

1 In a large bowl layer cauliflower, broccoli, green onions, radishes, and carrot; set aside.

2 In a small bowl stir together mayonnaise, sugar, lemon juice, horseradish, salt, and pepper; spread over vegetables. Sprinkle with bacon. Cover and chill for 4 to 24 hours. Before serving, toss to coat vegetables.

Makes 8 to 10 servings

Per serving: 267 cal., 25 g total fat (4 g sat. fat), 20 mg chol., 409 mg sodium, 10 g carbo., 3 g fiber, 4 g pro.

To tote: *Transport in an insulated cooler with ice packs.*

Garlic Roasted Vegetable Salad

New potatoes, green beans, garlic, rosemary, and balsamic vinegar combine for a vegetable salad you'll crave after the bowl is long empty.

Prep: 20 minutes   **Roast:** 1 hour   **Oven:** 400°F

- 8   oz. green beans, cut into 1½-inch pieces
- 1   head garlic
- 2   lb. tiny new potatoes, quartered
- 2   medium red sweet peppers, cut into large chunks
- 4   green onions, sliced
      Salt and black pepper
- ¼   cup chicken broth
- ¼   cup balsamic vinegar
- 2   Tbsp. olive oil
- 1   tsp. snipped fresh rosemary

1. Preheat oven to 400°F. Cook green beans in boiling water for 3 minutes. Drain; place in ice water to cool. Drain beans again; set aside.

2. Peel away the dry outer layers of skin from the head of garlic, leaving skins and cloves intact. Cut off the pointed top portion (about ¼ inch), leaving bulb intact but exposing tops of individual cloves.

3. Place the garlic head, cut side up, in a shallow roasting pan. Add green beans, potatoes, sweet peppers, and green onions. Sprinkle with salt and black pepper. Drizzle chicken broth over all. Roast, uncovered, about 1 hour. Cool slightly.

4. For dressing, squeeze out the garlic paste from individual cloves into a bowl; add vinegar, olive oil, and rosemary. Stir to combine. Transfer roasted vegetables to a bowl. Add dressing; toss to coat. Serve warm or cover and chill for 4 to 6 hours.

Makes 8 servings

Per serving: 143 cal., 4 g total fat (1 g sat. fat), 0 mg chol., 43 mg sodium, 25 g carbo., 4 g fiber, 4 g pro.

To tote: *Cover warm salad tightly. Transport warm salad in an insulated carrier. Transport chilled salad in an insulated cooler with ice packs.*

Sweet Potato Salad

A sweet potato salad will stand out on any potluck party table. Orange, ginger, honey, and nutmeg all flavor the mayonnaise dressing.

Prep: 40 minutes   **Chill:** 8 to 24 hours

4 lb. sweet potatoes, peeled and cubed

¼ tsp. salt (optional)

2 cups light mayonnaise dressing or salad dressing

2 Tbsp. finely shredded orange peel

⅔ cup orange juice

2 Tbsp. honey

½ tsp. grated fresh ginger or ⅛ tsp. ground ginger

¼ tsp. ground nutmeg

2 cups sliced celery

½ cup snipped dried apricots

1 cup chopped walnuts or pecans, toasted

1 cup canned pineapple tidbits, drained

1 In a Dutch oven combine sweet potatoes, salt (if desired), and enough water to cover. Bring to boiling; reduce heat. Simmer, covered, about 15 minutes or until potatoes are just tender. Drain well and cool slightly.

2 Meanwhile, for dressing, in a very large bowl combine mayonnaise dressing, orange peel, orange juice, honey, ginger, and nutmeg. Stir in celery and apricots. Add cooked potatoes; toss lightly to coat. Cover and chill for 8 to 24 hours.

3 Just before serving, stir in nuts and pineapple.

Makes 16 to 20 servings

Per serving: 270 cal., 15 g total fat (3 g sat. fat), 10 mg chol., 204 mg sodium, 34 g carbo., 4 g fiber, 3 g pro.

To tote: *Transport salad, nuts, and pineapple in an insulated cooler with ice packs.*

Fettuccine Vegetable Toss

For a pretty presentation, use spinach fettuccine and both red and yellow tomatoes. Topped with feta cheese, it's a dish you'll want to serve again and again.

Prep: 20 minutes   **Chill:** 4 to 24 hours

- 8 oz. dried spinach fettuccine or plain fettuccine
- 2 Tbsp. olive oil
- ¼ cup chopped green onions
- 2 cups chopped red and/or yellow tomatoes
- ½ cup finely chopped carrot
- ¼ cup oil-packed dried tomatoes, drained and snipped
- ⅔ cup crumbled garlic-and-herb, peppercorn, or plain feta cheese

1 Cook fettuccine according to package directions; drain. Rinse with cold water; drain again. Transfer fettuccine to a large serving bowl; toss with half of the olive oil.

2 Meanwhile, in a large skillet heat the remaining olive oil over medium heat. Add green onions; cook and stir 30 seconds. Stir in fresh tomatoes, carrot, and dried tomatoes.

Cover and cook for 5 minutes, stirring once. Spoon tomato mixture and feta cheese over cooked fettuccine; toss gently. Cover and chill for 4 to 24 hours.

Makes 8 servings

Per serving: 179 cal., 6 g total fat (2 g sat. fat), 8 mg chol., 124 mg sodium, 25 g carbo., 1 g fiber, 6 g pro.

To tote: *Transport in an insulated cooler with ice packs.*

Broccoli-Cauliflower Bake

Cruciferous vegetables such as broccoli and cauliflower are packed with antioxidants and are high in fiber, vitamins, and minerals too.

Prep: 20 minutes   **Bake:** 20 minutes   **Oven:** 375°F

- 4 cups broccoli florets
- 3 cups cauliflower florets
- ½ cup chopped onion
- 1 Tbsp. butter or margarine
- 1 10.75-oz. can condensed cream of mushroom soup or cream of chicken soup
- 3 oz. American cheese or process Swiss cheese, torn
- ¼ cup milk
- ½ tsp. dried basil, thyme, or marjoram, crushed
- 1 cup soft bread crumbs
- 1 Tbsp. butter or margarine, melted

1 Preheat oven to 375°F. Cook broccoli and cauliflower, covered, in a small amount of boiling lightly salted water for 6 to 8 minutes or until vegetables are almost crisp-tender; drain. Remove broccoli and cauliflower from pan; set aside.

2 In the same saucepan cook onion in the 1 tablespoon hot butter over medium heat until tender, stirring occasionally. Stir in soup, cheese, milk, and basil. Cook and stir over medium-low heat until bubbly and cheese melts. Gently stir in broccoli and cauliflower. Transfer mixture to a 2-quart casserole. In a bowl toss together bread crumbs and the 1 tablespoon melted butter; sprinkle over vegetable mixture.

3 Bake, uncovered, about 20 minutes or until heated through.

Makes 8 servings

Per serving: 141 cal., 9 g total fat (4 g sat. fat), 19 mg chol., 506 mg sodium, 11 g carbo., 3 g fiber, 5 g pro.

Garlic and Pepper Stir-Fry

Nutty-flavor sesame oil has a high smoke point, which makes it excellent for high-heat stir-frying. Choose a light-color toasted sesame oil for this light and tasty side dish.

Start to Finish: 25 minutes

- ¼ cup soy sauce
- 2 tsp. toasted sesame oil
- ½ tsp. cracked black pepper
- 2 Tbsp. vegetable oil
- 6 cloves garlic, minced
- 4 medium red, yellow, and/or green sweet peppers, cut into bite-size strips
- 2 medium onions, sliced and separated into rings
- 4 cups sliced fresh mushrooms

  Toasted sesame seeds

1 For sauce, in a bowl combine soy sauce, sesame oil, and black pepper; set aside.

2 Pour oil into a large wok or an extra-large skillet; heat wok over medium-high heat. (Add more oil as necessary during cooking.) Add garlic; cook and stir for 1 minute. Add sweet peppers and onion rings; cook and stir for 3 minutes. Add mushrooms; cook and stir for 2 to 3 minutes more or until vegetables are crisp-tender.

3 Push vegetables from center of wok. Stir sauce; add to wok. Cook and stir until bubbly and vegetables are coated. Transfer mixture to a serving dish. Sprinkle with sesame seeds. Serve immediately.

Makes 8 servings

Per serving: 95 cal., 6 g total fat (1 g sat. fat), 0 mg chol., 464 mg sodium, 8 g carbo., 2 g fiber, 4 g pro.

Baked Butter Beans with Mustard

In the southern U.S., large dried lima beans, also called Fordhook beans, are often referred to as butter beans.

Prep: 20 minutes   **Bake:** 45 minutes   **Oven:** 325°F

- 8   slices bacon, diced
- 1   cup chopped onion
- 4   16-oz. cans butter beans and/or Great Northern beans, rinsed and drained
- 1   8-oz. carton sour cream
- ½   cup chicken or vegetable broth
- 1   Tbsp. all-purpose flour
- 1   Tbsp. snipped fresh rosemary
- 1   Tbsp. Dijon-style mustard
- ½   tsp. freshly ground black pepper
- 2   Tbsp. chopped Italian (flat-leaf) parsley
- 2   tsp. finely shredded lemon peel

1 Preheat oven to 325°F. In a skillet cook bacon over medium heat until crisp; remove bacon, reserving 1 tablespoon drippings. Drain bacon on paper towels; set aside. Cook onion in reserved drippings over medium heat until tender. Transfer onion to a bowl. Add drained beans and all but 2 tablespoons of the bacon; set aside.

2 In another bowl whisk together sour cream, broth, flour, rosemary, mustard, and pepper. Stir into bean mixture. Transfer to 2-quart casserole.

3 Bake, covered, for 45 minutes, stirring once halfway through. In bowl combine remaining bacon, parsley, and lemon peel; sprinkle on beans just before serving.

Makes 10 servings

Per serving: 247 cal., 10 g total fat (5 g sat. fat), 20 mg chol., 892 mg sodium, 26 g carbo., 6 g fiber, 12 g pro.

Swiss Vegetable Medley

Frozen vegetables are lifesavers in this quick-to-make side dish. Choose the mixture of vegetables you like best.

Prep: 15 minutes   **Bake:** 35 minutes   **Oven:** 350°F

- 2 16-oz. pkgs. frozen broccoli, cauliflower, and carrots, thawed
- 2 10.75-oz. cans condensed cream of mushroom soup
- 2 cups (8 oz.) shredded Swiss cheese
- ⅔ cup sour cream
- ½ tsp. black pepper
- 2 2.8-oz. cans french-fried onions

1 Preheat oven to 350°F. In a large bowl combine thawed vegetables, soup, half of the Swiss cheese, the sour cream, and pepper. Stir in half of the French-fried onions. Spoon vegetable mixture into a 3-quart rectangular baking dish.

2 Bake, covered, for 30 minutes. Uncover and sprinkle with the remaining cheese and remaining french-fried onions. Bake about 5 minutes more or until heated through.

Makes 12 servings

Per serving: 249 cal., 17 g total fat (6 g sat. fat), 22 mg chol., 589 mg sodium, 14 g carbo., 3 g fiber, 9 g pro.

To tote: *Cover tightly. Transport in an insulated carrier.*

Cheesy Brussels Sprouts with Bacon

Brussels sprouts—people either love them or they don't. Those who love them will adore this dish—and those who don't may change their minds.

Prep: 15 minutes   **Bake:** 20 minutes   **Oven:** 400°F

8   cups Brussels sprouts, quartered

3   slices bacon, diced

½   cup chopped onion

2   cloves garlic, minced

1   16-oz. jar Alfredo pasta sauce

1   cup soft bread crumbs

⅓   cup shredded Parmesan cheese

2   Tbsp. butter, melted

1 Preheat oven to 400°F. Cook Brussels sprouts in a small amount of lightly salted boiling water for 5 minutes (sprouts will not be tender); drain and keep warm.

2 Meanwhile, in an oven-going skillet cook bacon over medium heat until crisp; remove bacon, reserving drippings. Drain bacon on paper towels; set aside.

3 Add onion and garlic to skillet; cook until onion is tender. Add Brussels sprouts, bacon, onion mixture, and Alfredo sauce. Stir gently to coat.

4 In a bowl combine bread crumbs, Parmesan cheese, and melted butter. Sprinkle over top of Brussels sprouts mixture.

5 Bake, uncovered, for 20 to 25 minutes or until heated through and topping is golden.

Makes 8 servings

Per serving: 309 cal., 22 g total fat (10 g sat. fat), 51 mg chol., 817 mg sodium, 15 g carbo., 4 g fiber, 14 g pro.

Farm-Style Green Beans

Beans complete almost any entrée and this bright, crisp-tender side dish is a year-round favorite.

Start to Finish: 25 minutes

- 1 lb. fresh green beans, trimmed
- 4 slices bacon, diced
- 2 cups thinly sliced onions
- 1 cup fresh sliced mushrooms
- 3 cups chopped tomatoes
- ½ tsp. salt

1 Leave green beans whole or cut into 1-inch pieces. In a saucepan cook the beans in a small amount of boiling lightly salted water about 10 minutes or until crisp-tender; drain and keep warm.

2 Meanwhile, in a skillet cook bacon over medium heat until crisp. Remove bacon, reserving drippings. Drain bacon on paper towels; set aside.

3 Cook onion and mushrooms in the reserved drippings over medium heat until tender. Add tomatoes and salt. Cook, uncovered, 2 to 3 minutes or until most of the liquid has evaporated.

4 Transfer warm green beans to a serving bowl. Top beans with onion mixture and bacon.

Makes 8 servings

Per serving: 132 cal., 9 g total fat (3 g sat. fat), 13 mg chol., 312 mg sodium, 10 g carbo., 3 g fiber, 4 g pro.

Creamed Corn Casserole

Serve this family-friendly favorite to brighten the table any weeknight. Corn dishes are favorites for almost anyone.

Prep: 15 minutes   **Bake:** 45 minutes   **Stand:** 5 minutes   **Oven:** 375°F

Nonstick cooking spray

2 16-oz. pkg. frozen whole kernel corn

2 cups chopped red and/or green sweet peppers

1 cup chopped onion

1 Tbsp. butter or margarine

¼ tsp. black pepper

1 10.75-oz. can condensed cream of celery soup

1 8-oz. tub cream cheese spread with chive and onion or cream cheese spread with garden vegetables

¼ cup milk

1 Preheat oven to 375°F. Lightly coat a 2-quart casserole with cooking spray; set aside. Place corn in a colander and thaw by running under cold water; drain. Set aside.

2 In a large saucepan cook sweet peppers and onion in hot butter over medium heat until tender. Stir in drained corn and black pepper. In a bowl whisk together soup, cream cheese spread, and milk. Stir soup mixture into corn mixture. Transfer to prepared casserole.

3 Bake, covered, for 45 to 55 minutes or until heated through, stirring once. Let stand for 5 minutes before serving.

Makes 12 servings

Per serving: 176 cal., 9 g total fat (5 g sat. fat), 22 mg chol., 280 mg sodium, 22 g carbo., 3 g fiber, 4 g pro.

Fresh Vegetable Gratin

A gratin is a casserole that's topped with bread crumbs and cheese. Leeks, zucchini, and yellow summer squash create a delicious and healthful side dish.

Prep: 15 minutes   **Bake:** 20 minutes   **Oven:** 425°F

- 4 large leeks, trimmed and cut into ¼-inch slices (2 cups)
- 2 medium zucchini, cut into ¼-inch slices (2½ cups)
- 2 medium yellow summer squash, cut into ¼-inch slices (2½ cups)
- ¼ cup olive oil
- Salt and black pepper
- ½ cup fine dry bread crumbs
- ½ cup finely shredded Parmesan cheese
- 1 tsp. dried thyme, crushed
- 2 cloves garlic, minced

1 Preheat oven to 425°F. In a medium bowl combine leeks, zucchini, yellow squash, and 2 tablespoons of the oil. Sprinkle with salt and pepper. Transfer vegetables to an ungreased 2-quart square baking dish.

2 In a small bowl stir together bread crumbs, Parmesan cheese, thyme, garlic, and remaining 2 tablespoons oil. Sprinkle crumb mixture evenly over vegetables. Bake, uncovered, for 20 to 25 minutes or until vegetables are tender.

Makes 8 servings

Per serving: 144 cal., 9 g total fat (2 g sat. fat), 6 mg chol., 134 mg sodium, 11 g carbo., 2 g fiber, 5 g pro.

To tote: *Cover tightly. Transport in an insulated carrier.*

Test Kitchen Tip: *Unlike green onions, the long green tops of leeks are not tender and not recommended for cooking. To trim a leek, cut off and discard these green tops. Trim off roots from the white stalk. Remove and discard any outer layers of the white stalk that appear tough. Rinse the stalk to remove any dirt or sand. Slice the stalk crosswise. (If you notice bits of dirt between the white layers, rinse again.)*

Sweet Potato Casserole

If you love sweet potatoes, you'll enjoy this dish. Take it along to your next holiday gathering at Grandma's house. The pecan topper is wonderful!

Prep: 20 minutes   **Bake:** 35 minutes   **Oven:** 350°F

2   beaten eggs

½   cup granulated sugar

¼   cup butter or margarine, melted and cooled slightly

1   tsp. vanilla

½   tsp. salt

4   cups cooked, mashed sweet potatoes

½   cup raisins

½   cup packed brown sugar

¼   cup all-purpose flour

2   Tbsp. cold butter

½   cup chopped pecans

1 Preheat oven to 350°F. In a large bowl stir together the eggs, granulated sugar, melted butter, vanilla, and salt. Stir in the cooked sweet potatoes and raisins. Spread sweet potato mixture evenly in an ungreased 2-quart square baking dish.

2 For topping, in a small bowl combine brown sugar and flour.

Using a pastry blender, cut in the cold butter until mixture resembles coarse crumbs; stir in pecans. Sprinkle over sweet potato mixture. Bake, uncovered, for 35 to 40 minutes or until heated through.

Makes 8 servings

Per serving: 460 cal., 16 g total fat (7 g sat. fat), 78 mg chol., 282 mg sodium, 77 g carbo., 4 g fiber, 6 g pro.

To tote: *Cover tightly. Transport in an insulated carrier.*

Au Gratin Potatoes and Peas

Dill, cheddar cheese, and pimiento flavor this great-tasting potato dish. A cracker crumb topper adds the right crunch.

Prep: 35 minutes   **Bake:** 30 minutes   **Oven:** 350°F

1½	lb. potatoes, peeled and cut into ½-inch cubes
1	cup coarsely crushed rich round crackers or shredded wheat wafers
2	Tbsp. butter or margarine, melted
⅓	cup butter or margarine
⅓	cup all-purpose flour
1	tsp. dried dill
¾	tsp. salt
¼	tsp. black pepper
2½	cups milk
1½	cups (6 oz.) shredded sharp cheddar cheese
1	16-oz. pkg. frozen peas, thawed
1	4-oz. jar diced pimiento, drained

1 Preheat oven to 350°F. In a large saucepan combine potatoes and enough water to cover. Bring to boiling. Cook, covered, for 3 minutes. Drain; set aside.

2 Meanwhile, grease a 3-quart rectangular baking dish; set aside. In a small bowl combine the crushed crackers and the melted butter; set aside.

3 For sauce, in a large saucepan melt the ⅓ cup butter. Stir in flour, dill, salt, and pepper. Add milk all at once. Cook and stir over medium heat until thickened and bubbly. Remove from heat. Add cheese, stirring until melted.

4 Combine potatoes, peas, and pimiento in prepared baking dish; pour sauce over all. Sprinkle with cracker mixture. Bake, uncovered, about 30 minutes or until potatoes are tender.

Makes 10 servings

Per serving: 322 cal., 18 g total fat (10 g sat. fat), 46 mg chol., 523 mg sodium, 30 g carbo., 4 g fiber, 11 g pro.

To tote: *Cover tightly. Transport in an insulated carrier.*

Best-Ever Potatoes

Two kinds of cheese, sour cream, and a tomato topper make these potatoes winners for any potluck.

Prep: 25 minutes   **Bake:** 30 minutes   **Oven:** 350°F

- 7 cups coarsely chopped small red potatoes
- 1 cup chopped onion
- 1 8-oz. carton sour cream
- 1 cup (4 oz.) shredded Monterey Jack cheese
- 1 cup (4 oz.) shredded sharp cheddar cheese
- ½ tsp. salt
- ¼ to ½ tsp. ground red pepper
- 2 medium tomatoes, seeded and chopped

1 Preheat oven to 350°F. In a large saucepan cook potatoes and chopped onion, covered, in a small amount of boiling water for 12 to 15 minutes or until tender; drain. Stir in sour cream, Monterey Jack cheese, cheddar cheese, salt, and red pepper. Stir in chopped tomatoes. Spoon into a 2-quart rectangular baking dish. Bake, uncovered, about 30 minutes or until heated through.

Makes 10 servings

Per serving: 214 cal., 12 g total fat (8 g sat. fat), 32 mg chol., 268 mg sodium, 19 g carbo., 2 g fiber, 9 g pro.

To tote: *Cover tightly. Transport in an insulated carrier.*

Cheesy Garlic Potato Gratin

Any chop, roast, or steak is even better with a great potato side dish. This one—rich with cheese and garlic—is one of the best.

Prep: 20 minutes **Cook:** 1½ hours **Stand:** 10 minutes **Oven:** 350°F

- 10 cups thinly sliced Yukon gold or other yellow-fleshed potatoes
- ⅔ cup sliced green onions
- 4 tsp. minced garlic
- 2 tsp. salt
- ½ tsp. black pepper
- 3 cups shredded Swiss cheese, provolone, or Jarlsberg cheese
- 2 cups whipping cream

1 Preheat oven to 350°F. Grease a 3-quart rectangular baking dish. Layer half of the sliced potatoes and half of the green onions in prepared dish. Sprinkle with half of the garlic, salt, pepper, and cheese. Repeat layers. Pour whipping cream over top.

2 Bake, covered, for 1¼ hours. Uncover and bake for 15 to 25 minutes more or until potatoes are tender when pierced with a fork and top is golden brown. Let stand for 10 minutes before serving.

Makes 12 servings

Per serving: 349 cal., 24 g total fat (15 g sat. fat), 85 mg chol., 470 mg sodium, 21 g carbo., 2 g fiber, 13 g pro.

Autumn Vegetable Pilaf

When sweet root vegetables marry with tender zucchini and fluffy rice, the result is a comforting cool-weather concoction.

Prep: 15 minutes   **Roast:** 15 minutes   **Oven:** 400°F

2   6- to 7.2-oz. pkg. rice pilaf mix

¼   cup olive oil

4   cloves garlic, minced

2   tsp. dried thyme, crushed

2   cups peeled and cubed sweet potatoes or carrots

2   medium zucchini, halved lengthwise and cut into ½-inch pieces

2   small red onions, cut into thin wedges

⅔   cup chopped pecans or walnuts, toasted

2   Tbsp. cider vinegar

1 Preheat oven to 400°F. Cook rice mix according to package directions, except omit butter or oil; keep warm.

2 Meanwhile, in a bowl stir together the oil, garlic, and thyme. Add sweet potatoes, zucchini, and onions, stirring to coat. Spread vegetables in a single layer in a large baking pan. Roast, uncovered, for 15 to 20 minutes or until vegetables are lightly browned and tender, stirring occasionally.

3 Stir vegetable mixture, nuts and vinegar into warm rice. Serve immediately.

Makes 12 servings

Per serving: 244 cal., 9 g total fat (1 g sat. fat), 0 mg chol., 349 mg sodium, 37 g carbo., 4 g fiber, 4 g pro.

Herbed Leek Gratin

Leeks practically melt into the marjoram-spiked sauce of this luxurious, subtly sweet side dish. It is super alongside roasted chicken and can bake in the oven at the same time.

Prep: 15 minutes   **Bake:** 35 minutes   **Oven:** 375°F

4½ lb. slender leeks

¾ cup whipping cream

¾ cup chicken broth

3 Tbsp. snipped fresh marjoram

¾ tsp. salt

¾ tsp. freshly ground black pepper

2¼ cups soft French or Italian bread crumbs

⅓ Tbsp. grated Parmesan cheese

⅓ Tbsp. butter, melted

Fresh marjoram sprigs (optional)

1 Preheat oven to 375°F. Trim roots off leeks, leaving pieces 4 to 5 inches long with white and pale green parts. Cut leeks in half lengthwise. Rinse leeks thoroughly by running under cold water; pat dry with paper towels. Arrange leeks, cut sides down, in a greased 3-quart rectangular baking dish, overlapping leeks as necessary to fit. (Leeks should all be facing the same direction.)

2 In a bowl combine whipping cream and chicken broth; pour over leeks. Sprinkle with half of the marjoram, the salt, and pepper. Bake, covered, for 20 minutes.

3 Meanwhile, in a bowl combine bread crumbs, Parmesan cheese, and remaining marjoram. Drizzle with melted butter; toss lightly to coat. Sprinkle bread crumb mixture over leeks.

4 Bake, uncovered, for 15 to 20 minutes more or until leeks are tender and crumbs are golden brown. If desired, garnish with fresh marjoram sprigs.

Makes 9 servings

Per serving: 237 cal., 15 g total fat (9 g sat. fat), 46 mg chol., 476 mg sodium, 23 g carbo., 2 g fiber, 4 g pro.

Focaccia Breadsticks

With refrigerated pizza dough, these enticing twists are amazingly easy to make. Serve them with pasta dishes or alongside minestrone, cheese, and vegetable soups.

Prep: 20 minutes   **Bake:** 12 minutes   **Oven:** 350°F

½ cup oil-packed dried tomatoes

½ cup grated Parmesan or Romano cheese

2 tsp. snipped fresh rosemary, crushed

¼ tsp. cracked black pepper

4 tsp. water

2 10-oz. pkg. refrigerated pizza dough

1 Preheat oven to 350°F. Lightly grease two large baking sheets; set aside. Drain dried tomatoes, reserving 4 teaspoons of the oil. Finely snip tomatoes. In a bowl combine tomatoes, cheese, rosemary, pepper, the reserved oil, and the water. Set aside.

2 Unroll pizza dough. On a lightly floured surface roll each portion of the dough into a 10×8-inch rectangle. Spread the tomato mixture crosswise over half of each rectangle.

3 Fold plain half of dough over filling; press lightly to seal edges. Cut each folded dough rectangle lengthwise into ten ½-inch strips, about 8-inches long. Fold each strip in half and twist two or three times. Place 1 inch apart on the prepared baking sheets.

4 Bake for 12 to 15 minutes or until golden. Immediately remove rolls from pans. Serve warm.

Makes 20 servings

Per serving: 84 cal., 2 g total fat (1 g sat. fat), 2 mg chol., 209 mg sodium, 14 g carbo., 1 g fiber, 3 g pro.

Cheddar-Corn Bread Rolls

Amaze your family by bringing a basket of homemade rolls to the table. This recipe makes it possible. These fluffy, cheese-studded rolls take less than an hour from start to finish.

Prep: 10 minutes **Rest:** 5 minutes **Rise:** 20 minutes **Bake:** 20 minutes per batch **Oven:** 375°F

2 16-oz. pkg. hot roll mix

2 cups shredded cheddar cheese

⅔ cup cornmeal

2½ cups hot water (120°F to 130°F)

¼ cup olive oil

2 eggs, lightly beaten

Milk

Cornmeal

1 In a bowl combine flour from the hot roll mixes, the contents of the yeast packets, the cheese, and the ⅔ cup cornmeal. Add the hot water, oil, and eggs; stir until combined.

2 Turn dough out onto a well-floured surface. Knead dough for 5 minutes or until smooth and elastic. Divide in half. Cover and let rest for 5 minutes. Lightly grease two 13×9×2-inch baking pans or baking sheets; set aside.

3 Divide each dough portion into 15 pieces. Shape each piece into a ball by pulling and tucking the dough underneath. Arrange 15 dough balls in each prepared pan. Cover and let rise in a warm place for 20 minutes.

4 Preheat oven to 375°F. Brush dough with milk and sprinkle with additional cornmeal. Bake, one pan at a time, for 20 to 22 minutes or until golden. Immediately remove rolls from pans. Cool on wire racks.

Makes 30 rolls

Per roll: 176 cal., 5 g total fat (2 g sat. fat), 22 mg chol., 228 mg sodium, 26 g carbo., 0 g fiber, 7 g pro.

Triple-Nut Zucchini Cake, page 265

Chapter 6

Most-Requested
Desserts

Peanut Butter Bars

This recipe is one to introduce kids to the joy of baking. The measurements are simple, patting the bottom layer into the pan is fun, and the result will make them proud.

Prep: 20 minutes **Bake:** 30 minutes **Cool:** 20 minutes **Oven:** 350°F

- 3 cups all-purpose flour
- 1 cup salted peanuts, finely chopped
- 1 cup sugar
- ¼ tsp. salt
- 1 cup peanut butter
- ¾ cup butter
- 2 tsp. vanilla
- 3 cups tiny marshmallows
- 1 cup semisweet chocolate pieces

1 Preheat oven to 350°F. Grease a 15×10×1-inch baking pan; set aside.

2 In a bowl stir together flour, peanuts, sugar, and salt. Using a pastry blender, cut in peanut butter and butter until crumbly. Stir in vanilla. Firmly pat 6 cups of the flour mixture into bottom of prepared pan.

3 Bake for 20 minutes. Top evenly with marshmallows, chocolate pieces, and remaining crumb mixture.

4 Bake for 10 to 15 minutes more or until marshmallows are toasted and crumbs are golden. Cool in pan on a wire rack for 20 minutes. Cut into bars (bars will be slightly crumbly).

Makes 32 bars

Per bar: 221 cal., 12 g total fat (5 g sat. fat), 11 mg chol., 104 mg sodium, 23 g carbo., 2 g fiber, 5 g pro.

Oat-Rhubarb Streusel Bars

In the United States rhubarb is often paired with strawberries. In Britain it appears more often with ginger, as it does here in these crumbly English-style bars.

Prep: 20 minutes   **Bake:** 55 minutes   **Cool:** 1 hour   **Oven:** 350°F

- 3   cups quick-cooking rolled oats
- 2   cups all-purpose flour
- 1½   cups packed brown sugar
- 1½   cups butter
- ½   cup granulated sugar
- ¼   cup all-purpose flour
- 1   tsp. ground ginger
- 4   cups fresh or frozen unsweetened sliced rhubarb
- 1½   cups powdered sugar
- ½   tsp. ground ginger
- ⅓   cup apricot nectar, orange juice, or milk
- 2   Tbsp. finely chopped crystallized ginger (optional)

1 Preheat oven to 350°F. Line a 13×9×2-inch baking pan with heavy foil, extending the foil over the edges of the pan; set aside.

2 In a bowl stir together oats, the 2 cups flour, and brown sugar. Cut in butter until mixture resembles coarse crumbs. Set aside 2 cups oats mixture. Press remaining mixture in prepared pan. Bake for 25 minutes. Remove from oven; set aside.

3 Meanwhile, in a bowl stir together granulated sugar, the ¼ cup flour, and the 1 teaspoon ground ginger. Add rhubarb; toss lightly to coat. Spread rhubarb mixture on partially baked crust. Sprinkle with reserved oats mixture; press lightly.

4 Bake for 30 to 40 minutes or until top is golden and filling is bubbly. Cool on a wire rack for 1 hour.

5 For icing, in a bowl combine powdered sugar and the ½ teaspoon ginger. Stir in apricot nectar.

6 Remove uncut bars from the pan, using the overlapping foil to lift. Place on cutting board; cut into bars. Drizzle icing and, if desired, sprinkle crystallized ginger over bars. Store, covered, in the refrigerator up to 2 days.

Makes 32 bars

Per bar: 221 cal., 10 g total fat (5 g sat. fat), 24 mg chol., 70 mg sodium, 32 g carbo., 1 g fiber, 2 g pro.

Super-Easy Chocolate Bars

Sweetened condensed milk in the filling for these bars is all the sweetener that's needed. These are decadently rich and satisfying.

Prep: 20 minutes   **Bake:** 35 minutes   **Oven:** 350°F

- 1   cup butter, softened
- ½   cup sugar
- ⅛   tsp. salt
- 2   cups all-purpose flour
- 1   14-oz. can (1¼ cups) sweetened condensed milk
- 1   cup semisweet chocolate pieces
- ½   cup chopped walnuts or pecans
- ½   tsp. vanilla

1 Preheat oven to 350°F. For crust, in a large mixing bowl beat butter with an electric mixer on medium to high speed for 30 seconds. Add sugar and salt; beat until combined, scraping sides of bowl occasionally. Beat in the flour on low speed until combined. Press two-thirds of the crust mixture into the bottom of an ungreased 13×9×2-inch baking pan.

2 For filling, in a medium saucepan combine sweetened condensed milk and chocolate. Stir over low heat until chocolate melts and mixture is smooth. Remove from heat. Stir in nuts and vanilla. Spread hot mixture over the crust. Dot with remaining crust mixture.

3 Bake about 35 minutes or until golden. Cool on a wire rack. Cut into squares.

Makes about 25 bars

Per bar: 213 cal., 13 g total fat (6 g sat. fat), 26 mg chol., 87 mg sodium, 24 g carbo., 1 g fiber, 3 g pro.

Candy Bar Cookies

Is it a cookie or candy? You decide. Either way, this treat is always a hit at potlucks and family gatherings.

Prep: 30 minutes   **Bake:** 10 minutes   **Oven:** 375°F

1	cup packed brown sugar
⅔	cup butter or margarine
¼	cup dark- or light-color corn syrup
¼	cup peanut butter
1	tsp. vanilla
3½	cups quick-cooking rolled oats
2	cups semisweet chocolate pieces
1	cup butterscotch pieces
⅔	cup peanut butter
½	cup chopped peanuts

1 Preheat oven to 375°F. Line a 13×9×2-inch baking pan with foil, extending foil over edges of pan; set pan aside. In a medium saucepan cook and stir brown sugar, butter, and corn syrup over medium-low heat until combined. Remove saucepan from heat; stir in the ¼ cup peanut butter and the vanilla until smooth.

2 For crust, place rolled oats in a very large bowl. Pour brown sugar mixture over oats, stirring gently until combined. Press oat mixture evenly onto bottom of prepared baking pan. Bake for 10 to 12 minutes or until edges are lightly browned.

3 Meanwhile, in the same saucepan cook and stir chocolate pieces and butterscotch pieces together over low heat until melted. Stir in the ⅔ cup peanut butter until mixture is smooth. Slowly pour mixture over the hot crust, spreading evenly; sprinkle with peanuts.

4 Cool in pan on a wire rack for several hours or until chocolate layer is firm. (If necessary, chill until chocolate is set.) When firm, use foil to lift out of pan. Cut into bars.

Makes 48 bars

Per bar: 166 cal., 9 g total fat (4 g sat. fat), 7 mg chol., 64 mg sodium, 16 g carbo., 2 g fiber, 3 g pro.

To tote: *Cover and transport in baking pan. (Or cut into bars and place in a single layer in a shallow container.)*

Chocolate Goody Bars

A fudge brownie mix shaves some prep time in the kitchen. The peanutty crunchy topping is spread over purchased vanilla frosting.

Prep: 20 minutes   **Bake:** 30 minutes   **Chill:** 1½ hours   **Oven:** 350°F

1 19.8-oz. pkg. fudge brownie mix

½ cup vegetable oil

2 eggs

¼ cup water

1 16-oz. can vanilla frosting

¾ cup chopped peanuts

2 cups semisweet chocolate pieces

1 cup creamy peanut butter

3 cups crisp rice cereal

1 Preheat oven to 350°F. Line a 13×9×2-inch baking pan with foil, extending foil over edges of the pan. Grease foil; set pan aside.

2 In a large bowl stir together the brownie mix, oil, eggs, and water. Spread batter in prepared pan. Bake for 30 minutes. Cool completely on a wire rack.

3 Frost bars with vanilla frosting. Sprinkle with peanuts. Cover and chill about 45 minutes or until frosting is firm.

4 Meanwhile, in a medium saucepan combine chocolate pieces and peanut butter. Cook and stir over low heat until chocolate is melted; stir in cereal. Spread over frosting. Cover and chill about 45 minutes more or until chocolate layer is set. Use foil to lift out of pan. Cut into bars. Store in the refrigerator.

Makes 36 bars

Per bar: 264 cal., 14 g total fat (4 g sat. fat), 12 mg chol., 140 mg sodium, 28 g carbo., 2 g fiber, 4 g pro.

To tote: *Cover and transport in baking pan in an insulated cooler with ice packs. (Or cut into bars and place in a single layer in a shallow container. Transport in an insulated cooler with ice packs.)*

Key Lime Cheesecake Bars

Fresh Key limes—small, round yellowish limes from Florida—may be hard to find, but the bottled juice or regular Persian limes are good substitutes in this fresh and zesty bar cookie.

Prep: 20 minutes   **Bake:** 30 minutes   **Cool:** 30 minutes   **Chill:** 4 hours   **Oven:** 350°F

2 cups finely crushed pretzel sticks

¼ cup sugar

1 cup butter, melted

4 8-oz. pkg. cream cheese, softened

1⅓ cups sugar

2 tsp. vanilla

6 eggs, lightly beaten

⅓ cup bottled Key lime juice or regular lime juice

1 tsp. finely shredded lime peel

½ cup chopped salted pistachio nuts

1 Preheat oven to 350°F. Line two 9×9×2-inch baking pans with foil, extending the foil about 1 inch over the ends of each pan. Lightly grease foil; set pans aside.

2 For crust, in a bowl combine crushed pretzels, the ¼ cup sugar, and the melted butter. Divide in half. Press each half evenly in each prepared baking pan. Bake for 10 minutes. Remove from oven; cool on a wire rack.

3 For filling, in a mixing bowl beat cream cheese, the 1⅓ cups sugar, and vanilla with an electric mixer until combined. Stir in eggs. Stir in lime juice and lime peel. Pour filling, dividing evenly, over each partially baked crust. Sprinkle each with pistachio nuts.

4 Bake for 20 to 30 minutes or until center appears set. Cool in pans on wire racks for 30 minutes. Cover and chill in the refrigerator for 4 to 24 hours (top will crack slightly). Remove from pans, using the overlapping foil to lift. Place on cutting board; cut into bars.

Makes 30 bars

Per bar: 254 cal., 19 g total fat (11 g sat. fat), 92 mg chol., 276 mg sodium, 17 g carbo., 0 g fiber, 4 g pro.

Cherry Cheesecake Bars

Maraschino cherries are the Queen Anne variety that have been macerated in almond-flavored sugar syrup. Their pretty color makes this recipe one to remember for Valentine's Day.

Prep: 25 minutes   **Bake:** 30 minutes   **Cool:** 1 hour   **Chill:** 4 hours   **Oven:** 350°F

- 2   cups (about 55 wafers) finely crushed vanilla wafers
- ⅓   cup butter, melted
- 1   10-oz. jar maraschino cherries
- 2   8-oz. pkg. cream cheese, softened
- 1   cup sugar
- 5   egg whites, slightly beaten

1 Preheat oven to 350°F. Line a 13×9×2-inch baking pan with foil, extending the foil about 1 inch over the ends of pan; set aside.

2 For crust, in a bowl combine crushed wafers and melted butter. Press mixture evenly in prepared pan. Bake for 10 minutes. Remove from oven; set aside.

3 Meanwhile, drain cherries well, reserving 2 tablespoons of the cherry liquid. If necessary, remove and discard stems from cherries. Finely chop the cherries; set cherries aside.

4 In a mixing bowl beat cream cheese and sugar with an electric mixer on medium speed until combined. Beat in reserved cherry liquid until combined. Stir in egg whites and chopped cherries.

5 Pour cream cheese mixture over partially baked crust, spreading evenly. Bake for 20 to 25 minutes or until set. Cool in pan on a wire rack for 1 hour. Cover and chill in the refrigerator for 4 to 24 hours. Remove from pans, using the overlapping foil to lift. Place on cutting board; cut into bars.

Makes 32 bars

Per bar: 157 cal., 9 g total fat (5 g sat. fat), 21 mg chol., 96 mg sodium, 18 g carbo., 0 g fiber, 2 g pro.

White Chocolate Brownies

For the best results and superb flavor when baking with white chocolate, choose a product that lists cocoa butter in its ingredients label.

Prep: 15 minutes **Bake:** 30 minutes **Cool:** 20 minutes **Oven:** 350°F

½   cup unsalted butter (no substitutes)

12   oz. white baking chocolate, coarsely chopped

4   eggs

1   cup sugar

2   cups all-purpose flour

1   tsp. salt

1   tsp. vanilla

2   cups semisweet chocolate pieces

1 Preheat oven to 350°F. Lightly grease a 13×9×2-inch baking pan; set aside. In a heavy saucepan heat and stir butter and half of the chopped white chocolate over low heat until combined. Remove pan from heat; set aside.

2 In a mixing bowl beat eggs with an electric mixer on medium to medium-high speed until thick and foamy. Gradually add sugar and beat about 3 minutes or until thickened. Add melted white chocolate mixture, flour, salt, and vanilla. Beat until just combined. Stir in the remaining chopped white chocolate and the chocolate pieces. Spoon mixture into a prepared pan.

3 Bake for 30 to 40 minutes or until evenly browned on top. Cool in pan on a wire rack for 20 minutes. Cut into bars.

Makes 40 bars

Per bar: 160 cal., 8 g total fat (5 g sat. fat), 29 mg chol., 76 mg sodium, 20 g carbo., 1 g fiber, 2 g pro.

Butterscotch Brownies

These buttery bars have the old-fashioned flavor of butterscotch combined with chunky nuts and melt-in-the-mouth marshmallows.

Prep: 20 minutes **Bake:** 15 minutes **Cool:** 20 minutes **Oven:** 350°F

⅓ cup butter
1⅓ cups coconut
¾ cup chopped pecans
⅔ cup packed brown sugar
½ cup butter, softened
1 cup packed brown sugar
½ tsp. baking soda
¼ tsp. salt
3 eggs
½ tsp. vanilla
1½ cups all-purpose flour
½ cup chopped pecans
½ cup tiny marshmallows
Caramel-flavored ice cream topping (optional)

1 Preheat oven to 350°F. Grease a 13×9×2-inch baking pan; set aside. In a saucepan melt the ⅓ cup butter over low heat; stir in coconut, the ¾ cup pecans, and the ⅔ cup brown sugar. Press evenly in prepared pan; set aside.

2 In a mixing bowl beat the ½ cup butter with an electric mixer on medium to high speed for 30 seconds. Add the 1 cup brown sugar, baking soda, and salt. Beat until combined, scraping sides of bowl occasionally. Beat in eggs and vanilla until combined. Add flour and beat until combined. Stir in the ½ cup pecans and marshmallows. Spoon small mounds of mixture over coconut mixture in pan. Carefully spread to cover.

3 Bake for 15 to 20 minutes (mixture should be evenly browned; center may jiggle slightly when shaken). Cool in pan on a wire rack for 20 minutes.

4 To serve, cut into bars. Drizzle with caramel topping.

Makes 24 bars

Per bar: 211 cal., 13 g total fat (6 g sat. fat), 43 mg chol., 113 mg sodium, 23 g carbo., 1 g fiber, 2 g pro.

Chocolate Dreams

These puffy domes with three chocolates and buttery-rich macadamia nuts are delightful. Serve them to your sweetheart or when you crave delicious chocolate.

Prep: 35 minutes   **Bake:** 8 minutes   **Oven:** 350°F

8	oz. bittersweet chocolate, chopped
2	Tbsp. butter
3	Tbsp. all-purpose flour
¼	tsp. baking powder
2	eggs
⅔	cup sugar
1	tsp. vanilla
2	cups chopped macadamia nuts
1½	cups semisweet chocolate pieces

1 In a saucepan cook and stir bittersweet chocolate and butter over low heat until melted and smooth. Remove pan from heat and cool mixture about 20 minutes.

2 Preheat oven to 350°F. Line two large cookie sheets with foil or parchment paper; set aside.

3 In a bowl combine flour and baking powder; set aside. In a mixing bowl beat eggs, sugar, and vanilla with an electric mixer on medium speed about 5 minutes or until mixture is thickened and pale yellow. Gently stir in flour mixture and cooled chocolate. Gently stir in macadamia nuts and chocolate pieces.

4 Immediately, using a small cookie scoop (1½ inches in diameter), drop dough in mounds 1 inch apart onto prepared cookie sheets. (Dough will thicken as it stands.)

5 Bake both sheets of cookies at the same time on separate racks for 8 to 9 minutes or until edges are set but centers are soft, switching sheets to the opposite racks halfway through baking. Cool cookies completely on cookie sheets set on wire racks. Peel cooled cookies off the foil or parchment paper.

Makes 40 cookies

Per cookie: 132 cal., 10 g total fat (4 g sat. fat), 12 mg chol., 11 mg sodium, 12 g carbo., 1 g fiber, 1 g pro.

Lime Zingers

Butter, lots of it, makes these zesty shortbread rounds utterly rich, tender, and delectable.

Prep: 40 minutes   **Bake:** 8 minutes per batch   **Oven:** 350°F

- 2   cups butter, softened
- 1   cup granulated sugar
- 4   tsp. finely shredded lime peel
- ½   cup lime juice
- 2   tsp. vanilla
- 4½   cups all-purpose flour
- 1½   cups finely chopped Brazil nuts or hazelnuts (filberts)
- 1   8-oz. pkg. cream cheese, softened
- 2   cups powdered sugar
- 2   Tbsp. lime juice
- 2   tsp. vanilla
       Finely shredded lime peel (optional)

1 Preheat oven to 350°F. In a mixing bowl beat butter with an electric mixer on medium to high speed for 30 seconds. Add the granulated sugar. Beat until combined, scraping sides of bowl occasionally. Beat in the 4 teaspoons lime peel, ½ cup lime juice, and 2 teaspoons vanilla until combined. Beat in as much of the flour as you can with the mixer. Using a wooden spoon, stir in any remaining flour and the nuts. Divide dough into fourths.

2 On a lightly floured surface, roll one-fourth of the dough at a time until ¼ inch thick. To roll, start from the center and push dough out toward the edges until it is a uniform thickness. Cut dough into rounds using a 2-inch cookie cutter. Place cutouts 1 inch apart on ungreased cookie sheets.

3 Bake for 8 to 10 minutes or until edges are light brown. Transfer to a wire rack and let cool.

4 For frosting, in a mixing bowl combine cream cheese, powdered sugar, the 2 tablespoons lime juice, and 2 teaspoons vanilla. Beat with an electric mixer on medium speed until smooth. Spread frosting on cooled cookies. If desired, sprinkle with additional lime peel.

Makes 84 cookies

Per cookie: 62 cal., 4 g total fat (2 g sat. fat), 9 mg chol., 31 mg sodium, 6 g carbo., 0 g fiber, 1 g pro.

Frosted Walnut Cookies

Shelled walnuts should be plump, meaty, and crisp. To keep nuts at their prime, store them, tightly covered, in the refrigerator up to 6 months.

Prep: 40 minutes   **Bake:** 10 minutes per batch   **Oven:** 375°F

½   cup shortening
1½ cups packed brown sugar
1   tsp. baking soda
½   tsp. baking powder
½   tsp. salt
2   eggs
1   tsp. vanilla
2½ cups all-purpose flour
1   8-oz. carton sour cream
⅔   cup chopped walnuts
⅓   cup butter, softened
4   cups powdered sugar
¼   cup milk
1½ tsp. vanilla
    Chopped walnuts or walnut halves (optional)

1 Preheat oven to 375°F. Grease a cookie sheet; set aside.

2 In a mixing bowl beat shortening with an electric mixer on medium speed for 30 seconds. Add brown sugar, baking soda, baking powder, and salt. Beat until combined, scraping sides of bowl occasionally. Beat in eggs and the 1 teaspoon vanilla until combined. Add flour and sour cream alternately to sugar mixture, beating until combined after each addition. Stir in the ⅔ cup nuts.

3 Drop dough by rounded teaspoons 2 inches apart onto the prepared cookie sheet. Bake for 10 to 12 minutes or until edges are light brown. Transfer to a wire rack and let cool.

4 For frosting, in a mixing bowl beat butter with 2 cups of the powdered sugar. Beat in milk and 1½ teaspoons vanilla until smooth. Gradually beat in the remaining 2 cups powdered sugar. If necessary, beat in additional milk to make spreading consistency.

5 Spread frosting on cooled cookies. If desired, top with additional walnuts.

Makes 60 cookies

Per cookie: 105 cal., 5 g total fat (2 g sat. fat), 13 mg chol., 63 mg sodium, 14 g carbo., 0 g fiber, 1 g pro.

Crunchy Caramel Apple Cake

Make this chunky cake with any apple you enjoy eating out of hand. Granny Smith, Gala, Honey Crisp, and Sonja varieties all shine in this recipe.

Prep: 25 minutes   **Bake:** 40 minutes   **Cool:** 1 hour   **Oven:** 325°F

1   cup plain granola, crushed
1   cup chopped walnuts or pecans
¼   cup butter, softened
3   cups all-purpose flour
1   tsp. baking soda
1   tsp. ground cinnamon
½   tsp. salt
2   eggs, lightly beaten
1½ cups vegetable oil
1   cup granulated sugar
1   cup packed brown sugar
3   cups finely chopped, peeled apples
½   cup butter
1   cup packed brown sugar
½   cup whipping cream
1   tsp. vanilla
    Whipped cream (optional)
    Chopped walnuts (optional)

1 Preheat oven to 325°F. Grease a 13×9×2-inch baking pan; set aside. In a bowl combine granola and ½ cup of the nuts. Use your fingers or a fork to combine the ¼ cup softened butter with granola mixture until crumbly; set aside.

2 In a bowl combine flour, baking soda, cinnamon, and salt; set aside. In a bowl combine eggs, oil, granulated sugar, and the 1 cup brown sugar. Add flour mixture; stir just until combined. Fold in apples and remaining nuts (mixture will be thick). Spoon batter into prepared pan, spreading evenly. Sprinkle with granola mixture.

3 Bake for 40 to 55 minutes or until a wooden toothpick inserted near the center comes out clean. Cool cake in pan on a wire rack for 1 hour.

4 For sauce, in a saucepan melt the ½ cup butter over medium heat. Stir in the 1 cup packed brown sugar and whipping cream. Bring to boiling, stirring constantly; reduce heat. Simmer, uncovered, for 5 minutes or until mixture is slightly thickened. Remove from heat; stir in vanilla. Cool sauce about 10 minutes before serving. Serve warm over cake. If desired, top with whipped cream and sprinkle with chopped nuts.

Makes 16 servings

Per serving: 630 cal., 39 g total fat (10 g sat. fat), 61 mg chol., 240 mg sodium, 68 g carbo., 3 g fiber, 6 g pro.

Marble Cake

This cake will go quickly! The rich chocolate frosting is sublime. Toffee bars, although optional, make a nice contrast of crunch to the creamy frosting.

Prep: 30 minutes   **Bake:** 30 minutes   **Cool:** 2 hours   **Oven:** 350°F

- 3 cups all-purpose flour
- 2½ tsp. baking powder
- ¾ tsp. baking soda
- ¼ tsp. salt
- ¾ cup butter, softened
- 2 cups sugar
- 1 Tbsp. vanilla
- 3 eggs
- 1½ cups milk
- ½ cup chocolate-flavored syrup
- 1 recipe Chocolate Butter Frosting
- 2 1.4-oz. bars chocolate-covered English toffee, chopped (optional)

1 Preheat oven to 350°F. Grease a 13×9×2-inch baking pan; set pan aside. Combine flour, baking powder, baking soda, and salt; set aside.

2 In a large mixing bowl beat butter for 30 seconds. Add sugar and vanilla; beat until fluffy. Add eggs, one at a time, beating well after each. Add flour mixture and milk alternately to beaten mixture, beating on low speed after each addition just until combined.

3 Transfer 1½ cups of the batter to a medium bowl; stir in chocolate-flavored syrup. Pour light batter into the prepared pan. Spoon chocolate batter over light batter. Gently cut through batters to marble.

4 Bake for 30 to 35 minutes or until a wooden toothpick comes out clean. Cool in pan on a wire rack. Frost with Chocolate Butter Frosting. If desired, sprinkle with chopped candy bars.

Makes 16 servings

Chocolate Butter Frosting: In a large mixing bowl beat 6 tablespoons butter and ½ cup unsweetened cocoa powder with an electric mixer on medium speed until fluffy. Gradually add 2 cups sifted powdered sugar, beating well. Slowly beat in ¼ cup milk and 1½ teaspoons vanilla. Slowly beat in an additional 2 cups sifted powdered sugar. If necessary, beat in additional milk to reach spreading consistency. Makes 2 cups.

Per serving: 453 cal., 16 g total fat (9 g sat. fat), 79 mg chol., 332 mg sodium, 74 g carbo., 1 g fiber, 5 g pro.

To tote: *Cover and transport in baking pan.*

Best-Ever Chocolate Cake

Look no farther. This absolutely perfect, decadent delight earns its name.

Prep: 20 minutes   **Bake:** 35 minutes   **Cool:** 1 hour   **Oven:** 350°F

¾	cup butter
3	eggs
2	cups all-purpose flour
¾	cup unsweetened cocoa powder
1	tsp. baking soda
¾	tsp. baking powder
½	tsp. salt
2	cups sugar
2	tsp. vanilla
1½	cups milk
1	cup semisweet chocolate pieces
¼	cup butter
½	cup sour cream
2½	cups powdered sugar
	Ice cream (optional)
	Fresh raspberries (optional)

1 Allow the ¾ cup butter and eggs to stand at room temperature for 30 minutes. Preheat oven to 350°F. Lightly grease a 13×9×2-inch baking pan; set aside. In a bowl combine flour, cocoa powder, baking soda, baking powder, and salt; set aside.

2 In a mixing bowl beat softened butter with an electric mixer on medium speed for 30 seconds. Gradually add sugar, beating until well combined. Scrape sides of bowl; continue beating on medium speed for 2 minutes more. Add eggs, one at a time, beating well after each addition. Beat in vanilla.

3 Alternately add flour mixture and milk to butter mixture, beating on low speed after each addition just until combined. Beat on medium to high speed for 20 seconds more. Spread batter into the prepared pan.

4 Bake for 35 to 40 minutes or until a wooden toothpick inserted near centers comes out clean. Cool in pan on a wire rack for 1 hour.

5 For frosting, in a saucepan heat and stir chocolate pieces and the ¼ cup butter over low heat until combined. Remove from heat; cool for 5 minutes. Stir in sour cream. (Mixture may be slightly warm when powdered sugar is added.) Gradually add powdered sugar, about ½ cup at a time, beating with an electric mixer on low speed until smooth. Frost the top of the cake. Store cake, covered, in the refrigerator for up to 1 week. If desired, serve with ice cream and fresh raspberries.

Makes 12 servings

Per serving: 360 cal., 15 g total fat (7 g sat. fat), 88 mg chol., 335 mg sodium, 51 g carbo., 1 g fiber, 6 g pro.

Carrot Cake

With carrot cake, cream cheese frosting is a must. What a way to get your vegetables!

Prep: 20 minutes   **Bake:** 40 minutes   **Cool:** 2 hours   **Oven:** 350°F

2   cups all-purpose flour
2   cups sugar
2   tsp. baking powder
1   tsp. ground cinnamon
½   tsp. baking soda
3   cups finely shredded carrots
1   cup vegetable oil
4   eggs
1   cup chopped pecans
1   recipe Cream Cheese Frosting

1 Preheat oven to 350°F. Grease a 13×9×2-inch baking pan; set pan aside. In a large mixing bowl stir together the flour, sugar, baking powder, cinnamon, and baking soda. Add finely shredded carrots, cooking oil, and eggs. Beat with an electric mixer until just combined. Stir in chopped pecans. Spread batter in prepared pan.

2 Bake for 40 to 45 minutes or until a wooden toothpick comes out clean. Cool in pan on a wire rack. Frost with Cream Cheese Frosting. Cover and store in the refrigerator.

Makes 16 to 24 servings

Cream Cheese Frosting: In a medium mixing bowl beat together 6 ounces cream cheese, softened, and 2 teaspoons vanilla with an electric mixer until light and fluffy. Gradually add 2 cups sifted powdered sugar, beating well. Gradually beat in 2 to 2½ cups additional sifted powdered sugar to reach spreading consistency. Makes about 1½ cups frosting.

Per serving: 481 cal., 24 g total fat (5 g sat. fat), 65 mg chol., 145 mg sodium, 65 g carbo., 2 g fiber, 5 g pro.

To tote: *Transport in an insulated cooler with ice packs.*

Banana Split Cake

Imagine all your favorite sundae flavors in a cake! Serve this cozy indulgence slightly warm to garner the most oohs and ahhs.

Prep: 20 minutes   **Bake:** 35 minutes   **Cool:** 30 minutes   **Oven:** 350°F

1   cup butter
4   eggs
3   cups all-purpose flour
2   tsp. baking powder
1   tsp. salt
¼   tsp. baking soda
1½   cups sugar
½   cup mashed ripe banana
½   cup sour cream
½   cup milk
1   tsp. vanilla
½   cup strawberry preserves
     Few drops red food coloring
½   cup presweetened cocoa powder (not low-calorie)
1   cup chocolate fudge ice cream topping
     Sliced bananas (optional)
     Fresh strawberries (optional)
     Whipped cream (optional)
     Maraschino cherries (optional)

1 Allow butter and eggs to stand at room temperature for 30 minutes. Preheat oven to 350°F. Grease and flour a 13×9×2-inch baking pan; set aside. In a bowl stir together flour, baking powder, salt, and baking soda; set aside.

2 In a mixing bowl beat butter with an electric mixer on low to medium speed for 30 seconds. Gradually add sugar, beating until well combined. Scrape sides of bowl. Add eggs, 1 at a time, beating well after each addition. In a bowl combine banana, sour cream, milk, and vanilla. Alternately add flour mixture and banana mixture to butter mixture, beating on low speed after each addition just until combined.

3 In a small bowl stir together 1 cup of the batter, the strawberry preserves, and red food coloring. In another bowl stir together another 1 cup of the batter and the cocoa powder. Spread all of the plain batter evenly into the prepared pan. Spoon chocolate and strawberry batters into small mounds randomly over the plain batter. Use a narrow metal spatula to gently swirl the batters.

4 Bake for 35 to 45 minutes or until a wooden toothpick inserted near center comes out clean. Cool in pan on a wire rack for 30 minutes.

5 In a saucepan heat ice cream topping just until drizzling consistency. If desired, serve cake with bananas, strawberries, whipped cream, maraschino cherries, and ice cream topping.

Makes 16 servings

Per serving: 410 cal., 17 g total fat (11 g sat. fat), 87 mg chol., 359 mg sodium, 60 g carbo., 1 g fiber, 4 g pro.

Triple-Nut Zucchini Cake

Make this ooey-gooey treat in midsummer, when zucchini plants are producing generously.

Prep: 25 minutes   **Bake:** 30 minutes   **Broil:** 1½ minutes   **Cool:** 2 hours   **Oven:** 350°F

¾   cup chopped walnuts

¾   cup chopped pecans

¾   cup slivered almonds, chopped

¾   cup rolled oats

2   cups all-purpose flour

2   cups granulated sugar

1   tsp. baking powder

1   tsp. salt

¼   tsp. baking soda

3   cups shredded zucchini

1   cup vegetable oil

3   eggs, lightly beaten

1   tsp. vanilla

⅓   cup butter

3   Tbsp. half-and-half, light cream, or milk

⅔   cup packed brown sugar

1 Preheat oven to 350°F. Grease a 13×9×2-inch baking pan; set aside. In a 15×10×1-inch baking pan combine ½ cup of the walnuts, ½ cup of the pecans, ½ cup of the almonds, and the oats. Bake about 12 minutes or until toasted, stirring three times. Set aside on a wire rack.

2 In a bowl combine flour, granulated sugar, baking powder, salt, and baking soda. Stir in zucchini, oil, eggs, and vanilla until combined. Stir in toasted nut mixture. Spread batter evenly in prepared pan.

3 Bake for 30 to 40 minutes or until a wooden toothpick inserted near the center comes out clean. Cool in pan on a wire rack for 1 hour.

4 In a saucepan heat and stir butter and half-and-half over low heat until butter melts. Add brown sugar; stir until sugar dissolves. Remove from heat. Stir in the remaining walnuts, pecans, and almonds.

5 Preheat broiler and carefully adjust oven rack so cake will be 4 to 5 inches from heat. Spread nut mixture over cake in pan. Broil for 1½ to 2 minutes or until topping is bubbly and golden. Cool in pan on a wire rack for 1 hour before serving.

Makes 20 servings

Per serving: 386 cal., 24 g total fat (5 g sat. fat), 41 mg chol., 182 mg sodium, 42 g carbo., 2 g fiber, 4 g pro.

Tiramisu

This classic Italian dessert is great for two reasons: It can be made up to 24 hours in advance, and it tastes so good you won't have to worry about toting home leftovers.

Prep: 30 minutes **Chill:** 4 to 24 hours

- ½ cup strong coffee
- 2 Tbsp. coffee liqueur
- 2 8-oz. cartons sour cream
- 2 8-oz. pkg. cream cheese, softened
- ⅔ cup sugar
- ¼ cup milk
- ½ tsp. vanilla
- 2 3-oz. pkg. ladyfingers, split
- 2 Tbsp. unsweetened cocoa powder

1 Combine coffee and coffee liqueur; set aside. In a large mixing bowl combine sour cream, cream cheese, sugar, milk, and vanilla. Beat with an electric mixer on high speed until smooth.

2 Layer one package of the ladyfingers, cut sides up, in a 2-quart rectangular baking dish; brush with half of the coffee mixture. Spread with half of the cream cheese mixture. Repeat with remaining ladyfingers, coffee mixture, and cream cheese mixture. Sift cocoa powder over the top. Cover and chill for 4 to 24 hours. To serve, cut into squares.

Makes 15 servings

Per serving: 248 cal., 18 g total fat (11 g sat. fat), 66 mg chol., 134 mg sodium, 18 g carbo., 0 g fiber, 4 g pro.

To tote: *Cover tightly. Transport in an insulated cooler with ice packs.*

Pineapple Cake

A coconut-pecan topping makes this pineapple cake stand out among similar versions. The topping becomes toasty and more flavorful during baking, yum!

Prep: 25 minutes   **Bake:** 30 minutes   **Oven:** 350°F

1	20-oz. can crushed pineapple
2½	cups all-purpose flour
1½	tsp. baking powder
½	tsp. baking soda
¼	tsp. salt
½	cup butter, softened
1	cup granulated sugar
2	eggs
¾	cup packed brown sugar
¾	cup chopped pecans
¾	cup coconut

1 Preheat oven to 350°F. Grease a 13×9×2-inch baking pan or a 3-quart rectangular baking dish; set aside. Drain pineapple, reserving juice. Combine flour, baking powder, baking soda, and salt; set aside.

2 In a large mixing bowl beat butter with an electric mixer on medium to high speed for 30 seconds. Add granulated sugar; beat until fluffy. Add eggs; beat until smooth. Add flour mixture and reserved pineapple juice alternately to beaten mixture, beating on low speed after each addition just until combined. Fold in pineapple. Spread batter in prepared pan.

3 Combine brown sugar, pecans, and coconut; sprinkle over batter. Bake for 30 to 35 minutes or until a wooden toothpick inserted in center comes out clean. Serve warm.

Makes 16 servings

Per serving: 285 cal., 12 g total fat (5 g sat. fat), 43 mg chol., 189 mg sodium, 43 g carbo., 1 g fiber, 3 g pro.

To tote: *Cover tightly. Transport in an insulated carrier.*

Triple Berry Pudding Cake

Having trouble deciding whether to bake berry shortcake, crisp, cobbler, or cake? This delectable dessert covers all the berry bases.

Prep: 25 minutes **Bake:** 40 minutes **Broil:** 1 minute **Cool:** 30 minutes **Oven:** 350°F

2	cups fresh or frozen blueberries, thawed
2	cups fresh or frozen raspberries, thawed
1	cup cranberries
2	cups all-purpose flour
1⅓	cups granulated sugar
3	tsp. baking powder
½	tsp. salt
1	cup milk
¼	cup butter, melted
2	tsp. vanilla
1½	cups boiling water
⅔	cup granulated sugar
1	cup sliced almonds
⅔	cup packed brown sugar
½	cup butter, melted

1 Preheat oven to 350°F. Grease a 13×9×2-inch baking pan. Arrange blueberries, raspberries, and cranberries in prepared pan; set aside.

2 In a bowl combine flour, the 1⅓ cups granulated sugar, baking powder, and salt. Add milk, the ¼ cup melted butter, and vanilla; stir well. Spoon batter over berries in pan; carefully spread batter over berries.

3 In a bowl combine the boiling water and the ⅔ cup granulated sugar; pour evenly over batter. Bake for 40 to 50 minutes or until top is browned and edges are bubbly.

4 Meanwhile, in a bowl combine almonds, brown sugar, and the ½ cup melted butter.

5 Remove cake from oven. Preheat broiler and carefully adjust oven rack so cake will be 4 to 5 inches from heat. Spoon almond mixture evenly over cake. Broil for 1 to 2 minutes or just until top is golden. Cool on a wire rack for 30 minutes before serving. Spoon warm pudding into dessert dishes.

Makes 16 servings

Per serving: 335 cal., 14 g total fat (5 g sat. fat), 25 mg chol., 194 mg sodium, 50 g carbo., 4 g fiber, 4 g pro.

Mini Almond Cheesecakes

These almond-crusted treats can be made well in advance and frozen individually. Sprinkle each bite-size dessert with a few slivered almonds.

Prep: 25 minutes   **Bake:** 18 minutes   **Chill:** up to 6 hours   **Oven:** 350°F

- ½ cup slivered almonds, toasted and ground
- 1 8-oz. pkg. cream cheese, softened
- ½ cup granulated sugar
- 1 egg
- ½ tsp. vanilla
- ½ tsp. almond extract
- ⅓ cup sour cream
- 2 Tbsp. powdered sugar
- ¼ tsp. vanilla
- ¼ cup slivered almonds, toasted

1 Preheat oven to 350°F. Grease twenty-four 1¾-inch muffin cups. Sprinkle about 1 teaspoon of the ground almonds into each cup. Gently shake so that almonds coat bottoms and sides of cups (do not shake out excess nuts). Set aside.

2 For filling, in a medium mixing bowl combine cream cheese and granulated sugar. Beat with an electric mixer on medium speed until smooth. Add egg, the ½ teaspoon vanilla, and almond extract. Beat until just combined. Spoon filling into prepared muffin cups, filling each three-fourths full.

3 Bake about 18 minutes or until tops just begin to turn golden. Cool in pans on a wire rack. Using a table knife, carefully loosen sides of cheesecakes from edges of cups. Carefully lift out of cups using the knife.

4 For topping, in a small bowl stir together the sour cream, powdered sugar, and the ¼ teaspoon vanilla. Spread topping on the cooled cheesecakes. Cover and chill up to 6 hours. Before serving, garnish each cheesecake with a few slivered almonds.

Makes 24 cheesecakes

Per cheesecake: 84 cal., 6 g total fat (3 g sat. fat), 20 mg chol., 32 mg sodium, 6 g carbo., 0 g fiber, 2 g pro.

To make ahead: *Freeze cheesecakes (without sour cream topping) in a single layer in a freezer container for up to 2 months. Thaw in the refrigerator overnight. Prepare and spread on the topping just before serving.*

To tote: *Place cheesecakes in a single layer in a covered container. Transport in an insulated cooler with ice packs.*

Praline Cheesecake Squares

As with most cheesecakes, this one is very rich and should be cut into small servings. Cheesecakes are best when served the day after baking.

Prep: 40 minutes   **Bake:** 50 minutes   **Chill:** 2 to 24 hours   **Oven:** 350°F

2½	cups all-purpose flour
1	cup butter, melted
⅔	cup finely chopped pecans
2	Tbsp. powdered sugar
3	8-oz. pkg. cream cheese, softened
4	eggs
1	14-oz. can sweetened condensed milk
⅔	cup granulated sugar
2	tsp. vanilla
1	cup packed brown sugar
1	cup whipping cream
1	cup chopped pecans
1½	tsp. vanilla

1 Preheat oven to 350°F. For crust, in a large bowl combine flour, melted butter, the ⅔ cup finely chopped pecans, and the powdered sugar; mix well. Press mixture into the bottom of a 13×9×2-inch baking pan. Bake for 15 to 20 minutes or until crust is set and light golden brown around the edges.

2 Meanwhile, for filling, in a large mixing bowl beat cream cheese with an electric mixer on low to medium speed until smooth. Add eggs; beat well. Beat in sweetened condensed milk, granulated sugar, and the 2 teaspoons vanilla. Pour filling over baked crust. Bake for 35 to 40 minutes until set. Cool in pan on a wire rack.

3 For topping, in a medium saucepan combine brown sugar and whipping cream. Cook and stir over medium heat until mixture boils; reduce heat. Simmer, uncovered, for 10 minutes. Remove from heat. Stir in the 1 cup chopped pecans and the 1½ teaspoons vanilla. Pour topping over cheesecake. Cover and chill for 2 to 24 hours before serving. Cut into squares.

Makes 48 squares

Per square: 214 cal., 15 g total fat (8 g sat. fat), 54 mg chol., 103 mg sodium, 18 g carbo., 1 g fiber, 3 g pro.

To tote: *Cover tightly. Transport in an insulated cooler with ice packs. (Or cut into squares and place in a single layer in a shallow container. Cover and transport in an insulated cooler with ice packs.)*

Strawberry Delight

This dessert is not too sweet, as some strawberry pies can be. Another time, substitute peaches when they are in season for strawberries, and peach gelatin instead of strawberry gelatin.

Prep: 30 minutes   **Bake:** 20 minutes   **Cool:** 30 minutes   **Chill:** 4 to 24 hours   **Oven:** 350°F

1½ cups all-purpose flour

¾ cup butter, melted

¾ cup chopped pecans

2 cups sifted powdered sugar

1 8-oz. pkg. cream cheese, softened

1 8-oz. carton frozen whipped dessert topping, thawed

3 cups sliced strawberries

1 cup granulated sugar

¼ cup all-purpose flour

3 Tbsp. strawberry-flavored gelatin

1 cup water

1 Preheat oven to 350°F. For crust, combine the 1½ cups flour and the melted butter; stir in pecans. Pat evenly in the bottom of a 3-quart rectangular baking dish. Bake about 20 minutes or until golden brown around edges. Cool in pan on a wire rack.

2 In a large mixing bowl beat powdered sugar and cream cheese with an electric mixer on medium speed until combined. Add whipped topping by spoonfuls; beat until smooth. Spread over cooled crust. Arrange sliced strawberries on top. Cover and chill while preparing top layer.

3 For top layer, in a medium saucepan combine granulated sugar, the ¼ cup flour, and the strawberry-flavored gelatin; stir in water. Cook and stir until thickened and bubbly. Cook and stir 1 minute more. Remove from heat. Cover surface and set aside to cool (about 30 minutes).

4 Spoon cooled gelatin mixture over strawberries. Cover and chill for 4 to 24 hours. Cut into squares.

Makes 15 servings

Per serving: 389 cal., 22 g total fat (12 g sat. fat), 43 mg chol., 152 mg sodium, 46 g carbo., 2 g fiber, 4 g pro.

To tote: *Transport in an insulated cooler with ice packs.*

Cherry Cobbler

Whip up this sweet classic when you crave a bowl of pure comfort. Fresh or frozen fruit makes the dessert easy to serve year-round.

Prep: 25 minutes   **Bake:** 20 minutes   **Oven:** 400°F

2   cups all-purpose flour

¼   cup sugar

3   tsp. baking powder

½   tsp. salt

¼   cup butter or margarine

12   cups fresh or frozen unsweetened pitted tart red cherries

2   cups sugar

¼   cup cornstarch

2   eggs, lightly beaten

½   cup milk

Vanilla ice cream (optional)

1 Preheat oven to 400°F. For topping, in a bowl combine flour, the ¼ cup sugar, the baking powder, and salt. Using a pastry blender, cut in butter until mixture resembles coarse crumbs; set aside.

2 For filling, in a saucepan combine the cherries, the 2 cups sugar, and the cornstarch. Cook over medium heat until cherries juice out, stirring occasionally. Cook and stir over medium heat until thickened and bubbly. Keep filling hot.

3 In a bowl stir together eggs and milk. Add egg mixture to flour mixture, stirring just to moisten. Transfer hot filling to a 3-quart rectangular baking dish. Using a spoon, immediately drop topping into twelve mounds over filling.

4 Bake, uncovered, for 20 to 30 minutes or until topping is golden brown. If desired, serve warm with ice cream.

Makes 12 servings

Per serving: 386 cal., 10 g total fat (5 g sat. fat), 58 mg chol., 236 mg sodium, 73 g carbo., 3 g fiber, 5 g pro.

Rhubarb Surprise Crisp

Spring's first treats—sweet strawberries and tart rhubarb—marry in a simple, old-fashioned dessert. Serve it slightly warm for the best effect.

Prep: 20 minutes   **Bake:** 30 minutes   **Oven:** 375°F

1⅓	cups granulated sugar
4	or 6 tsp. cornstarch
½	tsp. ground cinnamon
4	cups sliced fresh rhubarb or frozen unsweetened sliced rhubarb, thawed
4	cups coarsely chopped fresh strawberries
¼	cup snipped fresh basil
1	cup all-purpose flour
1	cup quick-cooking rolled oats
⅔	cup packed brown sugar
½	tsp. salt
⅓	cup butter, melted
	Sweetened whipped cream (optional)

1 Preheat oven to 375°F. In a bowl combine the granulated sugar, the cornstarch, and cinnamon. (For fresh rhubarb, use 4 teaspoons cornstarch. For frozen, use 6 teaspoons cornstarch.) Stir in rhubarb, strawberries, and basil. Spoon fruit mixture into a 3-quart rectangular baking dish, spreading evenly; set aside.

2 For topping, in another bowl combine flour, oats, brown sugar, and salt. Stir in melted butter. Sprinkle topping evenly over fruit mixture.

3 Bake, uncovered, for 30 to 40 minutes or until fruit is tender and topping is golden brown. Serve warm. If desired, top with sweetened whipped cream.

Makes 12 servings

Per serving: 281 cal., 7 g total fat (4 g sat. fat), 15 mg chol., 144 mg sodium, 54 g carbo., 3 g fiber, 3 g pro.

Blueberry Crisp

There is no better way to utilize blueberries in the summer months than with blueberry crisp. A scoop of vanilla ice cream adds to its perfection.

Prep: 20 minutes   **Bake:** 30 minutes   **Oven:** 375°F

3   Tbsp. all-purpose flour
2   Tbsp. granulated sugar
6   cups blueberries
¼   cup lemon juice
1   cup packed brown sugar
¾   cup all-purpose flour
¾   cup quick-cooking rolled oats
1¼ tsp. ground cinnamon
½   cup cold butter

1 Preheat oven to 375°F. In a large bowl stir together the 3 tablespoons flour and granulated sugar. Add blueberries and lemon juice; toss gently to combine. Spread berry mixture evenly in a 3-quart rectangular baking dish; set aside.

2 For topping, combine brown sugar, the ¾ cup flour, oats, and cinnamon. Using a pastry blender, cut in butter until mixture resembles coarse crumbs. Sprinkle topping evenly over berries.

3 Bake about 30 minutes or until topping is golden brown and edges are bubbly. Serve warm.

Makes 8 to 12 servings

Per serving: 371 cal., 13 g total fat (8 g sat. fat), 33 mg chol., 142 mg sodium, 63 g carbo., 4 g fiber, 4 g pro.

*****To tote:** *Cover tightly. Transport in an insulated carrier.*

Apple-Cranberry Dessert

Fresh cranberries are available only a short time, but they freeze beautifully. Buy a few extra bags and freeze them to use year-round.

Prep: 10 minutes **Bake:** 1 hour **Cool:** 30 minutes **Oven:** 325°F

- 2   12-oz. pkg. fresh cranberries
- 2   cups chopped, peeled, cored cooking apple
- 2   Tbsp. butter, cut up
- 1⅓ cups sugar
- 1   cup chopped walnuts or pecans
- 2   eggs, lightly beaten
- ⅔   cup butter, melted
- 1   cup sugar
- ⅔   cup all-purpose flour
- Vanilla ice cream

1 Preheat oven to 325°F. Grease the bottom of a 13×9×2-inch baking pan. Toss the cranberries and apple together in the prepared pan. Dot cranberry mixture with the 2 tablespoons butter. Sprinkle evenly with the 1⅓ cups sugar and the walnuts. Set aside.

2 In a bowl whisk together the eggs and the ⅔ cup melted butter. Stir in the 1 cup sugar and flour, whisking until well combined. Pour egg mixture evenly over cranberry mixture.

3 Bake, uncovered, about 1 hour or until top is golden brown and filling is bubbly. Cool on a wire rack for 30 minutes before serving. Serve warm or at room temperature with vanilla ice cream.

Makes 12 servings

Per serving: 540 cal., 27 g total fat (13 g sat. fat), 99 mg chol., 157 mg sodium, 72 g carbo., 4 g fiber, 6 g pro.

Index

Metric Information

The charts on this page provide a guide for converting measurements from the U.S. customary system, which is used throughout this book, to the metric system.

Product Differences

Most of the ingredients called for in the recipes in this book are available in most countries. However, some are known by different names. Here are some common American ingredients and their possible counterparts:

- Sugar (white) is granulated, fine granulated, or castor sugar.
- Powdered sugar is icing sugar.
- All-purpose flour is enriched, bleached or unbleached white household flour. When self-rising flour is used in place of all-purpose flour in a recipe that calls for leavening, omit the leavening agent (baking soda or baking powder) and salt.
- Light-color corn syrup is golden syrup.
- Cornstarch is cornflour.
- Baking soda is bicarbonate of soda.
- Vanilla or vanilla extract is vanilla essence.
- Green, red, or yellow sweet peppers are capsicums or bell peppers.
- Golden raisins are sultanas.

Volume and Weight

The United States traditionally uses cup measures for liquid and solid ingredients. The chart below shows the approximate imperial and metric equivalents. If you are accustomed to weighing solid ingredients, the following approximate equivalents will be helpful.

- 1 cup butter, castor sugar, or rice = 8 ounces = ½ pound = 250 grams
- 1 cup flour = 4 ounces = ¼ pound = 125 grams
- 1 cup icing sugar = 5 ounces = 150 grams

Canadian and U.S. volume for a cup measure is 8 fluid ounces (237 ml), but the standard metric equivalent is 250 ml.

1 British imperial cup is 10 fluid ounces.

In Australia, 1 tablespoon equals 20 ml, and there are 4 teaspoons in the Australian tablespoon.

Spoon measures are used for smaller amounts of ingredients. Although the size of the tablespoon varies slightly in different countries, for practical purposes and for recipes in this book, a straight substitution is all that's necessary. Measurements made using cups or spoons always should be level unless stated otherwise.

Common Weight Range Replacements

Imperial / U.S.	Metric
½ ounce	15 g
1 ounce	25 g or 30 g
4 ounces (¼ pound)	115 g or 125 g
8 ounces (½ pound)	225 g or 250 g
16 ounces (1 pound)	450 g or 500 g
1¼ pounds	625 g
1½ pounds	750 g
2 pounds or 2¼ pounds	1,000 g or 1 Kg

Oven Temperature Equivalents

Fahrenheit Setting	Celsius Setting*	Gas Setting
300°F	150°C	Gas Mark 2 (very low)
325°F	160°C	Gas Mark 3 (low)
350°F	180°C	Gas Mark 4 (moderate)
375°F	190°C	Gas Mark 5 (moderate)
400°F	200°C	Gas Mark 6 (hot)
425°F	220°C	Gas Mark 7 (hot)
450°F	230°C	Gas Mark 8 (very hot)
475°F	240°C	Gas Mark 9 (very hot)
500°F	260°C	Gas Mark 10 (extremely hot)
Broil	Broil	Grill

*Electric and gas ovens may be calibrated using celsius. However, for an electric oven, increase celsius setting 10 to 20 degrees when cooking above 160°C. For convection or forced air ovens (gas or electric), lower the temperature setting 25°F/10°C when cooking at all heat levels.

Baking Pan Sizes

Imperial / U.S.	Metric
9×1½-inch round cake pan	22- or 23×4-cm (1.5 L)
9×1½-inch pie plate	22- or 23×4-cm (1 L)
8×8×2-inch square cake pan	20×5-cm (2 L)
9×9×2-inch square cake pan	22- or 23×4.5-cm (2.5 L)
11×7×1½-inch baking pan	28×17×4-cm (2 L)
2-quart rectangular baking pan	30×19×4.5-cm (3 L)
13×9×2-inch baking pan	34×22×4.5-cm (3.5 L)
15×10×1-inch jelly roll pan	40×25×2-cm
9×5×3-inch loaf pan	23×13×8-cm (2 L)
2-quart casserole	2 L

U.S. / Standard Metric Equivalents

⅛ teaspoon	= 0.5 ml
¼ teaspoon	= 1 ml
½ teaspoon	= 2 ml
1 teaspoon	= 5 ml
1 tablespoon	= 15 ml
2 tablespoons	= 25 ml
¼ cup = 2 fluid ounces	= 50 ml
⅓ cup = 3 fluid ounces	= 75 ml
½ cup = 4 fluid ounces	= 125 ml
⅔ cup = 5 fluid ounces	= 150 ml
¾ cup = 6 fluid ounces	= 175 ml
1 cup = 8 fluid ounces	= 250 ml
2 cups = 1 pint	= 500 ml
1 quart	= 1 litre